THE REBELLION OF BOUDICCA

To war, this QVEEN doth with her Daughters moue,
She for her Wisdom, followed, They for Loue,
What Roman force, Such ioined powers could quell,
Before so murdering Charmes whole Legions fell.
Thrice happy Princess, had she rescued So
Her Doughters honour, and her Countrys too;
But they being ravish't, made her vnderstand
Tis harder Beauty to secure, then Land.
Yet her Example teaching them to dye
Virtue, the roome of Honour did Supply.

'Boadicea' from Aylett Sammes's Britannia Antiqua Restaurata

THE REBELLION
OF BOUDICCA

---

by

DONALD R. DUDLEY
M.A., F.S.A.

and

GRAHAM WEBSTER
M.A., Ph.D., F.S.A.

LONDON
ROUTLEDGE & KEGAN PAUL

First published 1962
by Routledge and Kegan Paul Limited
Broadway House, 68–74 Carter Lane
London, E.C.4

Printed in Great Britain
by W. & J. Mackay & Co Ltd, Chatham

© *D. R. Dudley & G. Webster 1962*

88

GENIO TERRAE BRITANNICAE

CONTENTS

CONTENTS

ILLUSTRATIONS

ix

Illustrations

(Plate I appears by courtesy of the Castle Museum, Norwich; plates II, VIII and XI of the British Museum; plate III of the National Museum of Wales; plates IVb, V, VI and VII of the Castle Museum, Colchester; plate X of S. S. Frere, Esq.; plates XII and XIII of W. A. Baker, Esq.).

PREFACE

AND ACKNOWLEDGEMENTS

'WHERE TWO GO TOGETHER', says the Greek proverb, 'the one sees before the other.' So it can be with the historian and the archaeologist, and the rebellion of Boudicca affords a notable opportunity for a joint exercise. The literary sources, if not so full as might be wished, are of a quality to capture the imagination of the poet and dramatist, as well as the historian. There is a good deal of archaeological evidence, and it is being added to; it is equally instructive to see where it fills the gaps in the 'historical' evidence and where it does not. The nineteen-hundredth anniversary of the rebellion therefore seems an occasion for a full review of the present state of our knowledge.

There is one other consideration we have had in mind. At the present time Roman Britain is enjoying an unprecedented vogue of popularity. This is a good thing in itself, but it brings its own dangers. Provincialism and insularity are the occupational risks of the student of Roman Britain, especially when it is approached as no more than an aspect of English local history. We have therefore tried to present the rebellion against the background of the Western provinces, and indeed of the Empire as a whole.

A full list of our obligations would be long indeed, but certain acknowledgements must be made here. First, to the East Anglian archaeologists, Lady Briscoe, Mr. Rainbird Clarke at the Norwich Museum, Mr. M. R. Hull at Colchester, and Mr.

Preface and Acknowledgements

Norman Smedley at Ipswich, who have treated invaders of their country with kindness and courtesy. The archaeological chapters have benefited from the advice of Mr. A. L. F. Rivet, and from that of Mr. Derek Allen on points of numismatics. Two Edinburgh scholars have given us the benefit of their expert knowledge, Professor K. H. Jackson on Celtic philology, and Dr. Ann Ross on Celtic religion. At Birmingham, Professor F. W. Shotton has given advice on geology, and in connexion with chapter 7, Professor T. J. B. Spencer has drawn attention to evidence in English literature unknown to us. We are grateful to the Librarian of the Royal Academy of Arts, Mr. Sidney Hutchison, and to Mrs. Elfrida Manning, for information about Thomas Thornycroft. Dr. Graham Webster also wishes to acknowledge the help of Miss Christine Johnson in reading the text of his chapters.

Finally, it should be said that chapters 3, 5, and 7 have been written by Professor Dudley, chapters 1, 2, and 6 by Dr. Graham Webster, while chapter 4 is a joint product.

Birmingham
September 1962

PLACE-NAMES

Littlechester	Derventio	St. Albans	Verulamium
London	Londinium		
		Thorpe-by-	Ad Pontem
Man, Isle of	Monavia Ins.	Newark	
Mancetter	Manduessedum	Tomen-y-Mur	not known
Margidunum	Castle Hill		
	(Notts.)	Venonae	High Cross
✓ Maryport	Alauna	Venta Icenorum	Caister St.
Metchley	not known		Edmunds
Mona	Anglesey	Venta Silurum	Caerwent
Moridunum	Carmarthen	Verulamium	St. Albans
Mons Graupius	not known	Villa Faustina	not known
		Viroconium	Wroxeter
Newstead	Trimontium		
Noviomagus	Chichester	Waddon Hill	not known
		(Dorset)	
Ratae	Leicester	Wall	Letocetum
Ribchester	Bremetennacum	Water Newton	Durobrivae
Richborough	Rutupiae	Worcester	not known
		Wroxeter	Viroconium
Silchester	Calleva	York	Eboracum

I

THE ICENI AND
THEIR NEIGHBOURS

IT USED TO BE THOUGHT that the prehistory of Britain was simple. There were the three ages of Stone, Bronze, and Iron, at the end of which (a little incongruously) a horde of woad-painted savages confronted Caesar's army. The mounting tide of new discoveries, and the reassessment of old ones, have swept all this away. The study of any period of British prehistory today faces more facts and problems than can be readily digested. In each region the pattern of cultural movements and cross-relationships becomes more complex. This is as true of East Anglia as most other parts of southern England, for the agrarian reforms of the eighteenth century which have made Norfolk famous have done much to obliterate traces of early man. Since Sir Cyril Fox made his fundamental studies, *The Archaeology of the Cambridge Region* and *The Personality of Britain*, no one need doubt the significance of geology and climate in determining the settlement pattern of prehistoric man. There is, however, another important factor which Fox established which has had a direct bearing on the origins of the Iceni—the relationship of East Anglia to the Continent. It is an area thrust boldly forward towards the mouth of the Rhine and north Germany. Peoples migrating from these areas would make a landfall on the coast of East Anglia, and it is hardly surprising to find cultural cross-connexions.

The geology of an area determines subsoil and vegetation. The effect on early man was profound, as he was not equipped

I

with the tools to deal with dense forests and tough clay land. The kind of subsoils he much preferred were the lighter sands and gravels, or barer chalk or limestone. Here he could clear the vegetation and scratch shallow furrows for planting his seeds. Until iron tools became cheap and plentiful this was the best he could do, so the thick woodlands supported by impervious clay subsoils remained almost untouched and unexplored, except for occasional hunting expeditions and incursions of grazing livestock. One can therefore trace effectively most of the settlement of man up to the end of the Iron Age by studying the subsoils. Here the map of solid geology is of little use. Much of Britain north of the Thames is covered by the detritus left by the succession of Ice Ages. Drift geology is a very difficult study, as the several deposits vary considerably within short distances. It is hardly surprising that the Geological Survey of Drift Sheets is not yet complete. Yet basically the geology of East Anglia is simple. Sweeping in a great curve towards the north-east is the broad chalk belt starting in Salisbury Plain and reappearing north of the Wash as the Lincolnshire Wolds. From the east of this to the coast the chalk disappears below the Norwich and Red Crags and Chillesford clays. Overlying the greater part of these rocks are vast areas of glacial deposit. The district known as High Norfolk, for example, is a layer of sticky clay 100 to 150 ft. thick, which caps the low plateau in the central area. On the north coast the Cromer Ridge of sand and gravel has created a strip of heathland. But the most interesting area is the Breckland, a tract of light sandy soil of some 250 square miles in west Norfolk and north-west Suffolk. Here the soil may even have been too light for extensive cultivation, but its grazing qualities alone would make it an important territory for early settlement. Unfortunately its close study is now made almost impossible by the extensive planting of conifers. However, we know it is particularly important, as it is connected to a thin strip of chalk which was not covered by boulder clay. This strip, only eight miles wide at its narrowest point, is the main land link with southern England. It was bounded on the west by the Fenlands, an area which up to the Roman conquest was uninhabitable except for various islands, great and small, which may have been welcome refuges for

Fig. 1. Geological Map of East Anglia.

hard-pressed peoples in those times, as they were in the early Middle Ages.

Here, then, is a general picture of the territory of the Iceni. To the north and east the boundary is the sea, with the rivers Waveney and Yare on the east, the Ouse from the Wash, offering access to sea-borne invaders. To the west was the protection of the Fens. Only to the south was there a land frontier to be defended. Most of this was covered by the dense forest of High Suffolk, the only link with reasonable access being the narrow chalk belt to the south-west. All this explains to a great extent the isolation of the Iceni, the failure of the Belgic pressure from the south to break through, and the fact that the Romans were content in the first few years of their occupation to leave on one side a client kingdom. Inside the territory the chalk strip, the Brecklands, and the sandy area to the north between Sandringham and Fakenham provided the main nuclei of settlement. But there were also suitable areas along the northern coastal fringe and the river terraces, and in particular the land to the west of Norwich. Probably half the total area was suitable for cultivation or pasture of varying quality. The southern boundary is difficult to define, and indeed may have changed through the period of the Iron Age. There is slight evidence of a contraction in the face of Belgic exploitation of the forest lands from the south, but this must be considered in its proper context.

The Iceni, like most of the British tribes, seem to have had mixed origins.[1] During the sixth and fifth centuries B.C. groups of people loosely associated with the Iron Age 'A' or Hallstatt culture were moving across into Britain from the Continent and colonizing the greater part of southern England and East Anglia. Earlier inhabitants still existing in a late Bronze Age culture were either absorbed or pushed into the marginal lands. These new peoples brought with them new styles in pottery and a knowledge of iron, but only small quantities of metal are normally found on their occupation sites. The knowledge was therefore still a secret craft of the wandering smiths who bartered these precious tools and weapons to the newcomers. A typical settlement of this period at West Harling in Norfolk has been discussed by Professor J. G. D. Clarke.[2] On a small gravel hill the excavators found remains of three houses, two of which were circular and the third rectangular in plan. The remains clearly indicate a farming economy with ox, sheep, horses, and dogs and wheat, while other bones of wild pig, red deer, and beaver showed that occasional hunting varied the diet. Weaving was indicated by the presence of spindle whorls, and flint scrapers could be associated with cleaning skins. One surprising thing was the complete absence of metal. It was too precious to lose, but antler handles suggest iron knives. On the other hand, there was a great quantity of pottery, and a study of the forms of vessels and their decoration traces these settlers back to the Netherlands. The settlement lasted for several generations, and they moved on, presumably, when the land became exhausted. A similar site has been described by Professor C. F. C. Hawkes at Runcton Holme,[3] but here the occupation, perhaps inter-mittently, went on into the Roman period. If the houses had been found it is more than likely that they would have changed but little from the early Iron Age form. This rural conservatism is clearly seen elsewhere in Britain as in the Cranborne Chase and adjacent areas.[4] Over the greater part of the Breckland, the chalk strip, and other suitable subsoils, there is evidence of similar native farmsteads. Only careful excavation will reveal their true nature; meanwhile they appear on the distribution maps merely as a scatter of pottery finds.

In the third and second centuries B.C., fresh influences came into the picture. These are represented by a spread of new ideas in pottery and, more impressive, finely decorated metalwork. These are the results of the so-called Marnian invasions. People from that part of France were certainly on the move. The sturdy farmers of Sussex resisted and forced the newcomers to seek a foothold elsewhere. One group went north to the Humber and founded a tribe known as the Parisi. They have been long known for their metalwork and in particular chariot burials and horse trappings.[5] Here it seems that a warrior aristocracy had established itself over a peasant population of earlier stock, as must have been happening all over the country at this time. The problem here is to distinguish objects left by this new aristo-cracy as settlers from those which may have been brought into the area by trade. Whether these Marnians would have brought their own smiths or whether these craftsmen would have moved from centre to centre making and selling their wares cannot be ascertained, but the new overlords with their love of finery and proud warrior traditions certainly created a market for bronze-smiths and jewellers.

Not so long ago it was thought that East Anglia was a remote poverty-stricken area which this new tide passed by.[6] But since the war the introduction of deep ploughing has brought to light an astonishing amount of rich metalwork which puts a new complexion on the Icenian story. Nor are these all merely objects introduced by trade, for the Shouldham sword was found with an inhumation burial.[7] This remarkable weapon with its anthropoid (i.e. having a human shape) hilt marks the burial of a Marnian warrior in this corner of north-west Norfolk. It shows that these invaders managed to obtain a foothold here and suggests that they might even have provided the Iceni with its aristocracy and in particular the ruling dynasty.

Much of the new metalwork has turned up in founders' hoards. They represent the scrap-metal a craftsman collected together in the course of his travels to provide him with the raw materials for his new work. Obviously he could not carry a large amount of metalwork about with him, so he usually buried it with great care in a place which he could easily find. If he died or was killed without telling anyone of his hoards, these remained buried until someone stumbled on them by accident. Today it is most often the ploughshare going a little deeper than usual that is responsible for their recovery. The most remarkable of these new discoveries is the Snettisham Treasure.[8] In a field at Ken Hill near this Norfolk village five hoards were found in 1948 and 1950 while the field was being ploughed. It is evident that originally all these objects belonged to one period and probably represented a number of near-by caches made by the original owner. Mr. R. R. Clarke reports that there are indications in the names of near-by fields that similar hoards may have been found in the Middle Ages. The importance of this find was not so much that it contained gold torcs of very unusual form and other torcs, bracelets, and rings, but also coins. There were thirteen gold coins found with the hoards and another was recovered by the British Museum laboratory from the terminal torc itself. Examples of these coins minted in Gaul had not previously been found in Britain much beyond the Thames basin. Although they were minted at the end of the first century B.C., the degree of wear indicates that the hoard must belong to a later period. There were also 116 coins made of speculum, an alloy of copper and tin, which are copies of the coinage of the Greek colony at Marseilles and date to the middle of the first century B.C. or perhaps later. The accepted date of deposition, considering both the coins and the metal objects, is about 25 B.C.–A.D. 10. (Pl. II).

The objects seem to be very much out of their context in north-west Norfolk, unless they represent the wanderings of a goldsmith from other parts of the country, whose establishment here was for the production of gold objects for the Icenian ruling house. This is an attractive idea, but Mr. R. R. Clarke has made another equally fascinating suggestion, that this represents some of the wealth of the rulers of the Trinovantes who sought refuge in Icenian territory when the Catuvellauni had invaded their kingdom and captured Colchester, its capital. In this case would the hoard be, as it quite evidently is, that of a goldsmith? On balance, the more prosaic idea may be nearer the truth.

After this remarkable discovery, the other items of metalwork seem rather insignificant. In 1950 a hoard of twelve bronzes was ploughed up at Ringstead,[9] only two or three miles from Snettisham. The objects include one of the finest bridle-bits ever found in Britain. Again this is a founder's hoard, buried somewhere in the middle of the first century B.C. It is this small area on the north-west corner of Norfolk which has produced not only these two hoards but two other single items of Iron Age metalwork.[10] This concentration of fine metalwork must be due to some local causes, and one cannot escape the conclusion that there was a suitable market in the form of aristocratic patronage.

The next significant stage in our chronology is the invasion of yet another people from the Continent, the Belgae, and with them we can move into historic times. Our information is derived from Julius Caesar, who tells us that these tribes, coming originally from Germany, settled in the northern parts of Gaul (Gallia Belgica), and within the memory of the Gauls of his day some of these Belgic people had crossed into Britain, first to plunder but later to colonize. Caesar's main concern was the help given by the British Belgae to their kinsmen in Gaul, and he felt that he could never conquer northern Gaul until he had put an end to this connexion. This is the main reason for his punitive raids into Britain in 55 and 54 B.C., which brought our islands for the first time into direct contact with Rome. Caesar came to do battle with the Belgae and in particular their chief Cassivellaunus. In his second expedition the great Roman general sought out the Belgae north of the Thames, and with the help of their neighbours the Trinovantes, Caesar found and captured the citadel of the Catuvellauni, which Sir Mortimer Wheeler has identified at Wheathampstead.[11] We thus know that by this time the Belgae had established themselves in Hertfordshire and that they had colonized Kent as well.

We learn more from Caesar about their economy and way of life, and archaeology helps to fill in the picture. The Belgae brought several new ideas into these islands. They made much more extensive use of iron for weapons and tools than their predecessors, and this not only gave them a superiority in warfare, but also enabled them to start to clear the dense woodlands and cultivate the heavy subsoil which hitherto had remained inviolate. Furthermore they made a distinctive pottery of fine quality and elegant shape on a fast wheel, probably using specialist craftsmen. These doughty warriors, said by Caesar to be the bravest of the Gauls, created a profound effect in Britain with their close-knit social integration and their industrious new agrarian economy. They soon recovered from their defeat by Caesar and began to threaten the Trinovantes in Essex. This latter tribe was also of Belgic origin and had settled perhaps at an earlier date on the light soils along the Essex and south Suffolk coast. The Trinovantes were protected by the Thames marshes and London clay belt from the south and south-west, and by the claylands of High Suffolk from the north-west, but rivers with their gravel terraces gave access directly towards the west and provided easy routes by which the Catuvellauni could infiltrate. The centre of the Trinovantian territory was the rich Colchester peninsula, a broad area of well-drained gravels flanked by the Colne and the Roman River. It was this area that the Catuvellauni coveted, mainly no doubt because it gave them easier access to the sea and the Continent than the route by the Thames, since this river was bordered for the most part by the heavy London clay which at that time supported thick forest.

Cassivellaunus had before Caesar's raids been moving in the Colchester direction, and the king of the Trinovantes had been slain in battle. His son Mandubracius had fled to Caesar for protection and help to regain his kingdom. Caesar was able to reinstate him and warn the Catuvellauni to leave the Trinovantes alone, and for a time at least they took heed. Under Tasciovanus, a successor of Cassivellaunus, the temptation became too great, especially, one suspects, with the growing prosperity of Camulodunum as an entrepôt for the trade with Gaul which was now beginning to flow into Britain in a regular stream. Round about 10 B.C., Tasciovanus was minting his coins in Camulodunum. He was the first prince of his line to place his name on the coins of the tribe, although it is difficult to deduce much from this. The introduction of coinage based on the Gallic models at least gives us a number of names of kings. Maps showing the distribution of types which can be identified with a particular tribe show the extent of its economic influence, and if there are sufficient coins, one may attempt to assess the actual area occupied by the tribe. Mr. Derek Allen [12] has shown that the success of Tasciovanus against the Trinovantes may have been shortlived, since there is another series of coins bearing the name of Addedomarus (as the first two D's of his name are barred, it may more correctly be rendered Athedomarus). The presence of this ruler minting at Camulodunum implies that the Trinovantes were in the ascendancy and were repelling the invaders from the west. Tasciovanus had for most of his reign to be content with Verulamium as his capital and mint.

Addedomarus was succeeded by Dubnovellaunus, who had connexions with Kent, east of the Medway. A study of his coin types suggests that he was ruling in Kent as a contemporary of Tasciovanus and succeeded to the Trinovantian dynasty either by kinship or conquest. He was, however, soon dispossessed by the new Catuvellaunian ruler who was to prove the greatest of them all, Cunobelinus.

Dubnovellaunus was forced to flee from Britain and his name as a suppliant king is found on the Roman inscription, known as the *Monumentum Ancyranum*.[13] But history was not to repeat itself, for Augustus was too preoccupied with his own problems to re-establish Dubnovellaunus as Caesar had Mandubracius. So Cunobelinus was able to consolidate his gains and soon launched a policy of dynamic expansion of his kingdom which had a profound effect on southern Britain. During the thirty years of his reign Cunobelinus endeavoured to advance his frontiers in all directions. The story can be partly seen in the distribution of his extensive series of coins. Kent fell to him, probably at an early stage. Later the powerful Atrebates, south of the Thames, were being ruled by Epaticcus, brother of Cunobelinus. He was probably established in place of the native king Verica, who was forced to flee, like others before him, to the protection of Rome. It has been suggested that this Verica is the same person as Bericus mentioned by the Greek historian Dio Cassius as an exile at the court of Claudius in A.D. 43.

There is another interesting facet of this dynastic struggle, brought out by Mr. Derek Allen and developed by Mr. C. E. Stevens.[14] The symbols on the coins of the two kingdoms of the Catuvellauni and Atrebates are the ear of barley and vine leaf respectively. It is not stretching the imagination too far to see in these the 'brand images', to use a modern phrase, of the anti- and pro-Roman parties in Britain. The vine leaf is associated with Mediterranean wine, then being imported into Britain in quantity, and the barley ear reflects the wealth of the Belgae, or their own potent brew of ale.

The pressure was also directed towards the west beyond the area of the spread of coins of the great king, for there is now archaeological evidence of the subjugation of the Dobunni in the Cotswolds by the Catuvellauni.[15] The chief centre at Bagendon, near Cirencester, is defended by Belgic-type earth-works and the pottery has very close affinities with that of Camulodunum.

The situation to the north in the shires of Leicester, Nottingham and Lincoln is still very imperfectly understood. It seems that the Coritani, whose tribal centre under Roman rule became Ratae (Leicester), were descendants of early Iron Age stock who had emigrated from Holland, probably via the Humber and Trent. Their culture, as revealed by Miss K. Kenyon's excavation on the Leicestershire hill-fort at Breedon,[16] and in 1960 by Mr. S. Thomas at the imposing hill-fort at Burrough-on-the-Hill near Melton Mowbray, shows complete lack of any Belgic influence. Only the presence of rotary querns is indicative of influence from the south. Although a Belgic settlement has been postulated [17] on the site of Leicester itself, the finds of pottery on which this is based could well have been introduced

Fig. 2. The Tribes of Britain.

by the Roman Army if, as seems likely, a Claudian fort was established here. Lincolnshire, on the other hand, presents a different picture, with a Marnian burial on the Wolds [18] and a fair number of important items of decorative metalwork, like the carnyx from Tattershall,[19] the famous Witham shield,[20] and the beautiful bronze scabbard-mount in the Lincoln Museum.[21] In 1961 an important new settlement site was discovered near Sleaford during the course of emergency excavations,[22] and this appears to be the centre of a Belgic enclave which may have included much of the eastern and central parts of Lincolnshire. Coin moulds were also found here showing that it was a mint of one of the centres producing the coinage formerly ascribed to the Brigantes, which now Mr. Derek Allen considers to be Corintanian.[23] The distribution of these coins, although not as conclusive as those denoting the territories of the other tribes, does indicate a Humber–Trent–Lincolnshire area of influence.

There may have been another important centre of Belgic influence at North Ferriby on the Humber, where pottery suggests a pre-Roman trading-post.[24] It is too early to say what these new discoveries mean in terms of Belgic penetration to the north-east and just how much effect this had on the Coritani. Another possibility is that there were several different tribes, and the coinage may belong to one whose name has been lost and whose lands may have been taken as the territory of the Lincoln *colonia*.

The north-western limits of Belgic influence may well be the Jurassic Way, a critical prehistoric watershed with possible [25] points of penetration like that at Wappenbury on the Leam in Warwickshire.[26]

The Iceni must have viewed with alarm the overthrow of the Trinovantes and the imperialistic designs of the Catuvellauni. But there was the protection of the thick forest of the central plateau, and the only line of advance was along the chalk strip between the trees and the fen. This clearly was the frontier and here the Belgic pressure must have been heavy. The great cross-dykes whose sharp profiles still dominate the landscape and which were once thought to have belonged to this period are now known to be of a later date, when the Saxons of Norfolk were defending themselves against their neighbours the Middle

Saxons. But a frontier post does exist at Wandlebury near Cambridge. At first sight this is not an impressive earthwork to one accustomed to those of the south or the Welsh borders. But it has been sadly mutilated in the building of an eighteenth-century shooting-box and stables, and by tree planting. Recent excavation[27] has shown that there were two main phases of construction and that the ditches and ramparts were of quite formidable size. Evidence has been produced which clearly indicates a state of neglect between the two phases. Only a small area of the interior was investigated, and until more is done it would be unwise to draw any definite conclusions. The excavation produced a considerable quantity of pottery, all of it early Iron Age and homogeneous in character, but its affinities seem to be with the Lower and Middle Thames area rather than Norfolk. Another surprising fact is the presence of a fair amount of iron work in the initial phase, which suggests that this cannot be too early in the period. Most important is the complete absence of any pottery or objects which could be associated with the Catuvellauni, and the inevitable conclusion reached by the excavator was that in its second phase Wandlebury was a border fort of the Iceni built against the Belgic intrusion. There was no evidence of any slaughter or destruction, but the Iceni may have fallen back to another line. Near the north coast of Norfolk, at Warham St. Mary, there is a circular fort very similar to Wandlebury, but in this situation it is difficult to see its purpose except as protecting a homestead of the local ruler.

The chalklands between Wandlebury and Newmarket are surprisingly bare of finds of this period, as if it was in truth a kind of frontier no-man's-land.[28] A discovery at Snailwell about two miles north of Newmarket may be an indication of Belgic penetration. This was an elaborate burial found in 1952.[29] The man had been laid in a sunken pit 6 ft. 6 in. by 9 ft. 6 in. in which a wooden structure, probably a sleeping-couch, occupied the greater part of the space and the rest was packed with all kinds of grave goods. There was a cremation burial at the bottom, and lying by it a remarkable bronze armlet ornamented at its terminals with beasts' heads, into which were set pieces of dark glass to represent the eyes. Other objects of personal use were a shield with a conical boss of Teutonic type, some bone toggles thought to be part of a harness, and a bronze bowl. There were also sixteen pottery vessels, including three large amphorae in which wine was imported, five flagons which probably contained other forms of liquid refreshment, four cups or beakers for drinking, two bowls, and a plate. All but two of these vessels are imports from Gaul, and the decoration of the couch is of uninspired Roman provincial workmanship. The pottery is very similar to examples from Colchester and Verulamium in a context dated to A.D. 10–50 and it is thus impossible to be sure it is pre-conquest. While an Icenian noble may have acquired all this pottery from traders, it seems unlikely that he would have adopted a Belgic type of burial, in contrast to the native inhumation still being practised. There are, however, at least two cremation burials well within Icenian territory at Elveden and Lakenheath,[30] and it may be that a change of custom was taking place at this critical time, and it was more likely to start with the aristocracy than with their subjects. Clearly we have not yet sufficient evidence to establish a Belgic penetration to the Lark, but the possibility remains. We are on more secure ground with the intrusion into the upper Stour Valley, but this was never important Icenian territory, and any occupation was restricted to the gravel river terraces.

Their coinage is an important source of information about the Iceni, and in particular their ruling house. Almost all the known coins of the Iceni have been found in thirteen hoards, ten of which have a very similar content. This suggests a serious threat at some time in the first century caused either by the Belgae or the Invasion or the disarming of the tribes in A.D. 48. Had these hoards belonged to the period of Boudicca they would have probably contained some Roman Imperial issues. The three exceptions do have these, one from Lakenheath includes issues of Caligula, and one from Stanton Downing of Claudius I, but the most important was found in 1961 at Joist Fen near Lakenheath. This contained three coins of a new type bearing an imitation Julio-Claudian head with the legend SVBI DASTO and a horse on the reverse with the word ESICO. Roman Imperial coins including some of Claudius I were also part of the hoard and this raises the question of native issue after A.D. 43. These new Icenian coins could however still have belonged to one of the last rulers or sub-rulers of the Iceni in pre-Roman times. The Icenian coins are degenerate copies of Catuvellaunian issues and show no originality. Some of them, however, bear names of rulers, usually just the beginning of the names, such as ANTED . . . who has been confused in the past with Antedrigus, a contemporary ruler of the Dobunni. Others are AESV . . . and SAEMV . . . which may be two versions of the same name, and in the letters ECEN . . . it is tempting to see the name of the tribe itself, but this is rare on coinage. There are other coins which bear the names CAMVL . . . and DVRO . . ., and it has been suggested that they were minted at Camulodunum. This has also been used as evidence that in a brief moment of glory the Iceni may have overrun and occupied Camulodunum. Another and more plausible explanation is based on the appearance of pairs of names which may be those of joint rulers or magistrates, a form of government common among the Gauls.[31] The absence of the name of Prasutagus from the coinage may seem surprising, but it would be explicable if he had been a Roman nominee, since he may not have been allowed to mint coins after his accession. The distribution of the Icenian coins strongly suggests that their economic influence was bounded by the River Lark and its southern tributary. (Pl. I.)

To complete this picture of the Iceni and their neighbours on the eve of the Roman invasion, something must be said about British methods of warfare. Information on the weapons and tactics used by the Britons against the Roman army can be derived from several sources. The most important accounts are by contemporary writers, but there are also sculptured reliefs on monuments, especially the triumphal arches in Gaul, showing the types of native weapons. These appear often as trophies captured during the battles and victories,[32] and had more of the Arch of Claudius in Rome survived one might have identified illustrations of British weapons. Warriors appear on British coins, but the details are usually inadequate.[33] Direct evidence comes in archaeological finds of weapons and equipment, but these are rare, they tend to suffer from corrosion, and their date is often doubtful. The description of Britain and the Celts generally by Strabo and Diodorus Siculus (Book V) was probably derived from several earlier writers, including Posidonius and Caesar.

The native ideas on fighting were those of the heroic age, as one would expect with a warrior class. In intertribal warfare the clash of individuals often decided the outcome rather than a general engagement. When the opposing sides had drawn up for battle, the warriors would step forward and challenge their opponents to single combat with boastful words. This provided both armies with a spectacle and satisfied the aspirations of the chief warriors. This type of warfare is typical of tribal feuds of all times, and can be seen as late as the Middle Ages, when the knights bore the brunt of the fighting. In its heroic form it can be seen in the Trojan War. But in more advanced societies, when circumstances and resources permit, an army may arise efficiently organized and equipped. If at the same time it is well led, then the heroic bands will be of little avail. It is this degree of organization, coupled usually with new tactical ideas, which is the secret of the success of most great armies. It explains the superiority of the Roman Army over the Celts, and later in history the Model Army created by Cromwell over King Charles's gentlemen soldiers.

The difference between the Roman and Celtic conception of warfare can be illustrated from their appearance and equipment. A Celtic chief was bedecked in martial trappings of barbaric splendour. Diodorus tells us of bronze helmets with large embossed figures, to which were fixed images of animals, anticipating perhaps the medieval crests. They also had highly decorated shields and wore iron body armour of plates and mail. Most of their followers had to be content with sword and buckler, going stripped into battle, and Caesar tells us of the Britons painting or tattooing their bodies to add to their ferocious appearance.

The splendid accoutrements of the warriors were a reflection of their wealth, and must have been jealously preserved and handed down through the generations like the equipment of the Japanese Samurai. We get occasional glimpses through rare finds, especially from river beds where, as lost objects, chance has preserved them in the mud. The horned helmet in the British Museum came from the Thames at Waterloo

Bridge, and there are also the two fine shields, one from Battersea, the other from the River Witham at Lincoln, both in the British Museum. These shields are remarkable examples of the craft of the bronze-smith and enameller, with the flowing curved designs used with such uninhibited skill, so soon to be lost in the tasteless, utilitarian era following the Roman invasion. Gallic coins often show standards in the form of a boar, but some of the British examples illustrate a horseman carrying a carnyx. This was a long trumpet with a mouthpiece in the shape of an animal's head. This remarkable instrument is well known from its appearance on the famous Gundestrup bowl,[34] but actual examples are very rare in Britain. A bronze boar's head found in 1816 in Banffshire has been identified by Professor Piggott[35] as an example of a mouthpiece, and a carnyx without its mouthpiece was found in the River Witham at Tattershall Ferry. These musical instruments must have played an important part in battle both in frightening the enemy and strengthening the morale of their own side, as well as giving simple commands and helping to rally the forces in case of a reverse.

The Gauls were also fine horsemen, and it was their cavalry which impressed Caesar. Here the gift for display and fine metal work is seen in the horse gear and trappings which are more commonly found than shields and helmets. Horsemen need long swords, and these well-fashioned weapons with their decorated scabbards show both beauty and variety.[36] With this barbaric display one must expect similar customs which may not accord with modern taste. The Celts, according to Posidonius, made a habit of cutting off the heads of their enemies and nailing them to their houses like hunting trophies. This is confirmed by illustrations on Trajan's Column of units of Gallic or British cavalry in the Roman army offering severed heads of Dacians to the Emperor. The practice of placing heads of traitors on town gateways survived into the Middle Ages, but its long ancestry may go back to this time. At the great Brigantian stronghold at Stanwick, the excavation carried out by Sir Mortimer Wheeler produced a skull which had been fixed to a pole by the entrance and had been subsequently lost in the ditch.[37] The more distinguished enemy heads, however, were carefully embalmed and preserved as heirlooms and doubtless shown to visitors as our family photograph album is today. (Pl. IV. A.)

In the techniques of war, Britain preserved a method of fighting which had become obsolete on the Continent. This was the use of the chariot, a vehicle which has been subject to much stupid antiquarian speculation, resulting in an entirely false picture which still survives in school history books. This distorted idea is best seen in the statue of 'Boadicea' on the Embankment, whose chariot has the appearance of an armoured milk-float. Caesar, who was intrigued by what was to him a novel method of fighting, has left us a detailed description of the British chariot and its method of use, but popular fancy, as usual, ignored the evidence. This is how Caesar describes the British chariots:

'In chariot fighting the Britons begin by driving all over the field hurling javelins, and generally the terror inspired by the horses and the noise of the wheels are sufficient to throw their opponents' ranks into disorder. Then, after making their way between the squadrons of their own cavalry, they jump down from the chariots and engage on foot. In the meantime their charioteers retire a short distance from the battle and place the chariots in such a position that their masters, if hard pressed by numbers, have an easy means of retreat to their own lines. Thus they combine the mobility of cavalry with the staying-power of infantry; and by daily training and practice they attain such proficiency that even on a steep incline they are able to control the horses at full gallop, and to check and turn them in a moment. They can run along the chariot pole, stand on the yoke, and get back into the chariot as quick as lightning.'

It is clear from this that the chariots must have been of very light construction with easy access at the front and rear. The idea of scythes fixed to the wheels dies hard, but this would have been thoroughly impracticable in Britain with its woods and thick undergrowth. It was a form of equipment used by the Parthians in the open desert, and even then the chariots would have been difficult to manipulate and easy to counter with rows of wooden stakes. Its main use was to create panic, however, and once the effect of surprise had gone the Romans held the chariot in contempt. A fourth-century Roman military inventor[38] revised the idea in the form of chariots with hinged scythes which could be raised and lowered by the occupants at will to enable the vehicle to proceed over rough ground, but like his other suggestions it was very fanciful, and the type of hinge which would have made the idea practicable is not discussed.

The basic shape of a Celtic war chariot is depicted on a coin of the Gallic tribe, the Remi, and a reconstruction was made possible by the discovery of fragments in the Llyn Cerrig Bach hoard, the significance of which is described below (p. 110). The model (Pl. III) which can now be seen in the National Museum of Wales was based on a study of the chariot by Sir Cyril Fox.[39] It is a remarkably small and light vehicle with a floor space of only 3 ft. square. The driver and warrior were protected by the two semicircular wicker screens at the sides, and the central pole with its double yoke for the two horses enabled the warrior to run along its length if necessary. The fragments of tyre from Llyn Cerrig were analysed and found equivalent to the finest Sheffield steel. The tyres were shrunk on to the wheel by heating them first, so that no nails were necessary. This is a good testimony of the skill of the British craftsman and blacksmith, and shows also the need for such high-quality work to take the severe strains imposed by the high speed and intricate manoeuvres of these chariots under battle conditions.

When the Britons engaged the Roman Army in a pitched battle they were never successful. We know of only five such instances. In four of these the ground was chosen by the Britons, and in the fifth case, against Boudicca, the Romans had the advantage of ground but were seriously outnumbered. But they were no easy victories. The first of them, the battle on the Medway, lasted two days, and only by an outflanking movement did the Romans eventually prevail. No one could doubt the qualities of courage and resolution possessed by the British warriors, but they lacked organization and training in warfare of the kind practised by the invaders. The Britons consisted of a loose collection of tribal levies each led by its own chief, and it would have been very difficult even under such a remarkable leader as Caratacus to have executed a simple tactical manoeuvre in the heat of battle without confusion resulting. The Roman command, however, was trained and disciplined precisely to this end. The enemy position was carefully explored: weaknesses found and exploited, and particular units advanced or detached accordingly. The Britons could deliver a surprise attack or plan a trap, but once engaged in the full fury of battle all was staked on attack or holding firm, although reserves would be held back for use at critical stages. Most of the infantry suffered, too, from lack of body armour, and once the legionaries moved into close quarters it rapidly became a massacre.

It was in small-scale guerilla warfare that the Britons excelled, since this was the kind of fighting to which they had become accustomed. Here the slow-moving Roman units were at a disadvantage, especially in wooded terrain. Caesar provides us with a graphic eyewitness account, during his second invasion, of fighting somewhere in Kent:

'The British cavalry and charioteers had a fierce encounter with our cavalry on the march, but our men had the best of it everywhere and drove them into the woods and hills, killing a good many, but also incurring some casualties themselves by a too-eager pursuit. The enemy waited for a time and then, while our soldiers were off their guard and busy fortifying the camp, suddenly dashed out of the woods, swooped upon the outpost on duty in front of the camp and started a violent battle. Caesar sent two cohorts—first of their respective legions—to the rescue, and these took up a position close together; but the men were unnerved by the unfamiliar tactics, and the enemy very daringly broke through between them and got away unhurt. That day Quintus Laberius Durus, a military tribune, was killed. The attack was eventually repulsed by throwing in some more cohorts. Throughout this peculiar combat which was fought in front of the camp in full view of everyone, it was seen that our troops were too heavily weighted by their armour to deal with such an enemy: they could not pursue them when they retreated, and dared not get separated from their standards. The cavalry, too, found it very dangerous work fighting the charioteers; for the Britons would generally give ground on purpose, and after drawing them some distance from the legions would jump down from their chariots and fight on foot, with the odds in their favour. In engaging their cavalry our men were not much better off; their tactics were such that the danger was exactly the same for both pursuers and pursued.

A further difficulty was that they never fought in close order, but in very open formation, and had reserves posted here and there; in this way the various groups covered one another's retreat, and fresh troops replaced those who were tired.'

Although we have no detailed accounts of the fighting in the later invasion period, it is clear that under suitable conditions the British tribes could be a serious menace to the Romans. During the governorship of Ostorius Scapula, in particular, in the difficult country to the west of the Severn, the Silures carried on for several years a highly successful guerilla campaign, inflicting serious damage on the Roman units established there. It was to end this state of affairs that Nero decided to conquer Wales, with the resulting campaigns under Veranius, Paulinus, and Frontinus.

2

THE ROMAN ARMY AND THE
MILITARY SITUATION
IN BRITAIN

THE TRIBAL LEVIES of the British *civitates* were faced by an enemy of an altogether different calibre. The Roman Army in Britain in the middle of the first century was a formidable force of well-equipped and disciplined men. At this period the main strength lay in its legions. There were four of these units, the IInd *Augusta*, IXth *Hispana*, XIVth *Gemina*, and XXth *Valeria*. The legion,[1] consisting of Roman citizens, was originally raised on a property qualification like that which governed the votes of British electors before the Reform Act. By the middle of the first century, recruitment was mainly from the more barbarized frontier districts and even citizenship became a legal formality easily surmounted by the recruiting officers. The legionaries were the heavily armoured foot soldiers whose equipment, organization, and discipline made them superior to their barbarian foes. They are seen on Trajan's Column, nearly fifty years later, each with his steel cuirass fitting in horizontal bands hinged at the back and fastened together at the front. Under this were back and front plates protecting the upper parts of chest and back and over which were worn the curved shoulder strips. This remarkable armour was extremely flexible and soldiers could wear it not only for fighting, but in digging ditches and building fortifications (as the Column shows). (Pl. IV.) On their heads they wore a well-designed helmet, but their legs were bare, protection here being sacrificed for mobility.

At this period it was essentially an attacking army. The function of the legions was to close rapidly with the enemy and use armour and disciplined manoeuvres to cut inroads into the barbarian hordes. The weapons of the legionary were the javelin and the sword. Each soldier carried two javelins, discharged in volleys on the attack at about forty and twenty yards. It was a cunningly designed weapon with a hardened steel point and soft iron shank fixed to its long wooden shaft. The idea, as Caesar himself tells us, was to disarm the enemy. As the volley of seven-foot javelins sailed through the air, the barbarians would instinctively put up their shields to take the impact. The hard point penetrated the wood or leather shield and the weight of the shaft bent the soft iron shank. Feverishly the warriors would try to pull the javelin out, but the point was firmly wedged; the seven-foot encumbrance made it impossible to use the shield, and it had to be cast aside. The armoured legions bore inexorably down upon their foe, only the chieftains of whom were still protected by their helmets. Once their shafts were discharged, the legionaries drew their short swords and closed their ranks. With their large semi-cylindrical shields pressed close to their bodies, their chins tucked well down, they moved at a gentle trot and, as a solid mass, smashed into the front ranks of the enemy, their short swords flicking rapidly into the soft parts of the foe and pushing them back by their very impact and weight. The barbarians may have been of heroic mould, but their prowess and skill were those of individuals; they had no defence against such an iron machine, superbly disciplined and controlled. Only by their very numbers, or by obstinacy in defeat, could they slow down or even stop the legions. Once the tide was turned and their morale cracked, they fled in mass panic, trampling down any waiting reserves.

At such a point in the battle the Roman commander swung his other units into action, the *auxilia*.[2] As the name implies, these men were intended to aid the legions. Originally, in Republican days, the sturdy Roman peasant made an excellent infantryman. Only men of property were expected to provide themselves with horses, and this gave rise to the *equites*, from which developed the equestrian order of Roman society. But they became the unit commanders rather than a body of cavalry. Very soon the Romans found themselves handicapped against other peoples who had perfected different kinds of warfare. There were the archers, slingers, and Celtic and eastern horsemen who had been nurtured in the saddle. Rome had, at an early date, to enlist the help of friendly allies or pay mercenaries to provide these specialist services in which she was so deficient. In this way these non-citizen allies came into being and gradually formed a permanent and indispensable part of the army. Augustus regularized the position and established the important principle that on completion of twenty-five years good and faithful service the auxiliaries should receive citizenship.

Whereas the legions were large units of five to six thousand men organized in centuries of eighty men and cohorts of six centuries, the *auxilia* were normally about five hundred strong, with exceptional units of one thousand. Another difference was that the legions were equipped in a standard way throughout the Empire, but each auxiliary unit was dressed in a manner traditional to the people from which it was first raised. Originally the allies would have brought their own weapons and armour as well as their methods of fighting. These would have become standardized in the early Empire, and although recruitment by then was no longer restricted to the country which had originally produced the unit, the appearance of the units remained the same. Just as today one finds Englishmen serving in the Scots Guards, so by the end of the first century Britons would be recruited into regiments of Gallic horse and Thracian infantry, and be drilled to the use of weapons and ways of fighting peculiar to these units.

There was in the *auxilia* a well-marked hierarchy; the senior service was the cavalry *alae* (literally 'wings'), the infantry cohorts were intermediate in status, while below them ranked the mixed regiment, the *cohortes equitatae*, partly infantry and partly mounted. There has always throughout history been a marked tendency for cavalry units to be proud, sometimes to the point of arrogance, and to become equipped in brilliant, occasionally bizarre finery. The Roman regiments were no exception. Trajan's Column clearly shows their beautifully groomed horses and ornate trappings. Many fragments of these have been found in excavations. The pendants of the first century were not only silvered but decorated with scroll and leaf patterns with black niello inlay, while the leather itself was highly ornamented with silver and gilt studs and complex patterns of different-coloured leather and cloth. The troopers themselves had two sets of equipment, one for fighting and one for parade. Today a British Army parade tends to be a rather stiff formal business of inspection and marching past a saluting-base. But there has still survived from more spacious and festive days such ceremonies as the Trooping of the Colour, where pageantry is closely integrated to the person of the sovereign and all the religious significance this entails. This in the feelings aroused may be compared with the parades of the Roman Army, in which religious ritual played an important part. What we may now lightly call superstition was for the great mass of the population of the classical world a matter of very life and death. There is little doubt that they held their beliefs very much at heart, and the whole success of campaigns might to them hinge on the whims of the gods. The due propitiation to win over the immortals became no stiff dull parade, but an anxious and thrilling moment for the soldiers.

A fragment of papyrus from the military archives at Dura Europos on the Upper Euphrates was found to be the official calendar of the *Cohors XX Palmyrenorum*[3] and lists most of the parade festivals in which this unit, with all others throughout the Roman Empire, would take part during the reign of Severus Alexander (A.D. 222–235). The number and complexity of these festivals is quite bewildering, and a study of this remarkable document leaves no doubt of the need for special parade equipment. The purpose behind all this was the continuity of the Imperial cult and the conditioning of non-Roman troops to Roman loyalties and traditions. We have a further glimpse of this aspect of military life in the treatise on tactics by Arrian, who was governor of Cappadocia during the reign of Hadrian.[4] He describes the cavalry on parade, 'The horsemen enter fully armed and those of high rank or superior in horsemanship wear gilded helmets. Unlike those made for active service, they do not merely cover the head and cheeks but are made to fit all round the face with apertures for the eyes. From the helmets hang yellow plumes which add to their beauty in the slightest breeze when the horses move. They carry oblong shields of a lighter type than those used in action, since both agility and smart appearance are the objects of the exercises, and the shields are improved by embellishments. Instead of breastplates, the horsemen wear tight leather jerkins embroidered with scarlet, red or blue and other colours; the horses have frontlets carefully made to measure and side-armour.' His further descriptions of their complicated manoeuvres reads like a detailed programme of the Royal Tournament, and shows that although there was this deep religious basis for the parades and festivals, the smartness of drill and glittering appearance were all calculated to improve morale and impress all others. Examples of the special parade helmets described by Arrian have been found in this country at Ribchester and Newstead, and one is seen on a tombstone at Cirencester.[5] But the richest discovery was made at Straubing in Austria, where there were several different types with eastern as well as classical head-dress and visor.[6] These were possibly for special festivals such as the Trojan Games, which were originally performed by boys on horseback.[7]

The infantry cohorts, led by a *praefectus cohortis*, were organized in centuries in the same way as the legion. They varied greatly in their equipment and tactics from lightly armed skirmishers to heavy infantry, and included such specialist arms as archers and slingers. The lowest grade, the mixed unit (*cohors equitata*), may be regarded as mounted infantry, but its precise function and organization is far from clear. Cheesman has pointed out the reference in Caesar to the Germans always having light infantry attached to their cavalry and fighting with them. So it is probable that such units would be organized like this when originally raised. Once they had established their usefulness in skirmishing and patrols which might otherwise have been carried out by the cavalry, they became an established part of the *auxilia*, though expendable in time of need. Hadrian clearly thought little of them; in his famous harangue he refers to one of these units thus, 'their appearance and condition of their weapons bears its relationship to the level of pay', although he then hastily praises their enthusiasm.

The Roman Army and the Military Situation in Britain

One of the problems to which it is not so easy to find a solution is the relationship of the *auxilia* to the legions in both the campaign and winter quarters. The first century saw a gradual change taking place as more responsibilities seemed to be moved over to the auxiliary arm. The brunt of the fighting had up to early Imperial times been borne by the legions. One has only to read Caesar's accounts of his campaigns to appreciate the reliance he placed on them. This is in contrast to the battle of Mons Graupius, where Agricola secured his victory entirely with his Batavian and Tungrian infantry, cavalry, and British levies, while the Twentieth Legion was held back as a reserve force. It is possible that Agricola was forced to use these tactics, as his army had by this stage in the advance been reduced to a very modest size and he needed his legions as an iron reserve if anything went wrong. This event clearly illustrates the dependence now placed on the *auxilia*, and as its logical development these units could be extensively employed in future campaigns and the legionary losses thereby reduced. The legionaries were also becoming valuable in other spheres, those of engineering and construction. The first century saw a great change in the accommodation for all units and the gradual evolution of the permanent timber-built fort, with its barrack blocks, headquarters, and other buildings, replacing the tented *hiberna*, reasonable perhaps in the warm Mediterranean winter, but intolerable in the northern snows and frost. Much of this new work of construction was undertaken by the legions, who received special training and equipment. These new skills and experiences must have created for the legions an enhanced value in the army, but it carried with it the seeds of decline. As the *auxilia*, especially the cavalry arm, undertook greater campaign responsibilities, so the legion shrank into mere garrison troops. But the warfare of later centuries (with its greatly changed factors) takes us beyond our immediate concern, the army of the first century in Britain.

A rather difficult matter to assess is whether auxiliary units were actually brigaded with legions at this period. The Roman frontier system with its network of forts, roads, signal stations, and depots as we know it in the second century in Britain and elsewhere took time to evolve. At the beginning of the Empire units were gathered into large winter quarters at selected points, and the idea of spreading them out to facilitate the control of a potentially hostile area did not come about rapidly. It may be that the army's experience in Britain hastened this development. Elsewhere the army had used large physical barriers such as the Rhine and Danube, or the deserts of North Africa or Syria. Across central England there was no such divide, but the Exe, Severn and Humber provided estuaries on which to anchor a frontier zone. None the less, how the units were disposed eludes us at present. At two of the legionary fortresses, Wroxeter and Gloucester, there is evidence of auxiliary units; in the former the actual fort south of the town and a tombstone, and in the latter a tombstone. But it is possible in both cases that the *auxilia* may have preceded the legions. Another problem arises out of the sizes of the fortress. Why is Lincoln only 42 acres and Chester as much as 59.3 acres? There are very few inscriptions which bracket legionaries and auxiliaries together, and these may refer merely to the units in a command area, just as the *diplomata* or discharge certificates may have been issued on this basis.

Service conditions and pay differed widely between the legions and *auxilia*. Legionaries were citizens when they joined the ranks and on retirement after twenty-five years' service received either a land grant in a colony or a lump sum donation, mainly from compulsory savings. The auxiliaries, on the other hand, received a discharge certificate granting them citizenship for themselves and their families. This steady increase in the franchise over the years, together with the block grants given from time to time to chartered towns and *civitates*, eventually led at the beginning of the third century to the famous edict of Caracalla granting citizenship to the greater part of the free population.[8]

The visible remains of any of the military sites in Britain of this period are extremely meagre. The reasons are simple; in the first place the structures themselves were of turf and timber and only the rampart and ditch system would have remained, and these were probably reduced by the unit before leaving the site. Also most of these forts are in the lowland parts of England, which since then have been subject to intensive cultivation. The plough by its long slow process of attrition has smoothed away the mounds and hollows and bitten deeply into occupation levels below the humus. If we had to rely entirely on a survey of the faint traces of these sites on the ground, our knowledge would be indeed slight. Fortunately there are always coins, pottery, and metal objects ploughed up and recognized which may direct attention to a particular locality. But most help has been gained through the development of aerial reconnaissance within the last few decades.

Seeing traces of banks and ditches in plan viewed from several hundred feet in the air enables one to recognize their significance in a way quite impossible on the ground. These impressions are strengthened when low sunlight casts long shadows over them and they spring into relief; the same effect is obtained after light snowfall. In light soils, there is a difference of colour over ditches and rampart after ploughing, dark where humus has filled in the ditches and light in the base of the rampart. But more telling and dramatic are the effects sometimes seen in the crops growing over ditches. The extra depth of humus creates a richer growth of crop, and this is accentuated in a spell of drought at the critical growing stage of the plant. When the crop on the rest of the field has ripened and turned yellow, that growing over the ditches remains green and shows up strongly from the air, but the effect may last only a day or so. (Pl. XII.) To catch these fleeting changes one has to fly over the fields at a short critical period. Moreover, the results are rarely noticed on clay subsoils, where the moisture content remains much the same everywhere. It is only in the light well-drained gravels and sands that one obtains the most striking effects. Fortunately these types of subsoil were those most favoured by the Roman Army commanders, because the vegetation was less dense and clearance a much easier task; in the wet weather any clay site under camp conditions quickly became a sticky morass. It has been through the continuous vigilance of such flyers as Dr. J. K. St. Joseph of Cambridge that we have so greatly added to our knowledge of the early military operations in Britain, and even more may be hoped for the future if the most productive areas are thoroughly surveyed each year.[9]

In studying these sites a distinction must be made between

the marching-camps and forts. The former are temporary positions housing a group of units in tents, as we would say 'under canvas', but the Romans *sub pellibus* (under leather). The tents were laid out in orderly rows with that of the commander in the centre, and the approximate density was about 550 men per acre. The tents were rectangular in shape, each holding eight men, and made of best calves' leather, stitched together in square panels. Round the camp a small ditch was dug about a yard deep and a yard square, and on the upcast was planted a row of palisade stakes tied together with thongs or withies. It was not meant to be a strong defensive barrier, but merely a fence to keep out wild animals and prevent the soldiers from straying. The Roman Army preferred to fight in the open, where it held all the advantages that training and discipline could give. Night fighting was almost unknown. These marching-camps can be recognized by the straight lines of the ditch meeting at right-angles in a well-rounded corner, and the gate openings usually protected by a short length of ditch dug in advance of it, or by a curved extension of the ditch. Unfortunately the temporary nature of the occupation rarely provides an excavation with any potsherds for dating.[10]

The forts, on the other hand, were much smaller and varied in size according to the type of holding unit. A cavalry regiment, for example, would need more room than an infantry one. As indicated elsewhere, the position in this period was fluid; the compact planning seen in the layout of the later forts is not present, and one must expect far more anomalies. There is evidence that two or more units were sometimes brigaded together, and this would necessitate forts of larger size. The internal arrangement follows in outline that of the marching-camp, but instead of tents there is an orderly array of timber barracks and other necessary buildings such as the headquarters block and granaries. One can even trace the outline of the tented arrangement in the plans of these buildings. They must have been of fairly simple construction, but it is only by their foundations that we know them at all. These foundations took various forms, but normally a narrow trench was dug, and in it laid a horizontal timber beam into which were slotted vertical uprights, or a similar trench could be used for convenient placing of upright posts unconnected with a beam. Alternatively a mere series of post-holes may be the only indication of the outline of the building. Above ground-level the builders must have covered the facing with weatherboarding or filled in the panels with wattle and daub. The roof was boarded or thatched. It is very rare that any of these constructional details survive. A destruction by fire may preserve some of the wood as charcoal, and fragments of baked clay daub with the pattern of wattles intact survive. The best preservation is found on a site which has been waterlogged since Roman times. In these conditions Professor Van Giffen, the Dutch archaeologist, was able to recover from Valkenburg the most remarkable details.[11] At present we know very little about these forts in Britain. Only at Hod Hill and in Holland at Valkenburg have the complete plans of any of them been recovered, and it would be unwise to generalize about them. They hold for the future an interest and importance in showing how the standard fort arrangements of the early second century gradually evolved from the tented *hiberna*.

The history of the invasion and early campaigns should now be considered in order that the arrangements of the units in A.D. 60 can be appreciated. The invasion of Britain took place in the summer of A.D. 43, with a strong force of four legions and *auxilia*, which embarked on the Channel and crossed with considerable reluctance. The legions were the IInd *Augusta*, IXth *Hispana*, XIVth *Gemina*, and XXth *Valeria*, under the command of a sound but scarcely dashing general, Aulus Plautius, with a carefully chosen staff. Either the Roman information was better than that of Caesar or the coastline had changed, for the main fleet anchored in a landlocked harbour at Richborough, on the tip of Kent. Ninety-seven years had passed since Roman troops had last disembarked on British soil. During that time many changes had taken place, but the Romans had always considered that the south-eastern part of Britain at least had been conquered. Now they were here to take over and make it into a province of the Empire. There had been maintained a process of diplomacy which deliberately sought to preserve friendly relationships with some of the British tribes.[12] That the Roman Army received help from these allies there seems little doubt, but in the histories dealing with the period no credit is allowed to them, triumphs and victories being for Roman arms alone.

After a single but substantial battle on the Medway,[13] the legions forced their way across by a turning movement on the flank led by Vespasian, then commander of the IInd *Augusta*. The main opposition had been from the Belgic tribes, which under their late King Cunobelinus had dominated much of southern and central England. Their power was now shattered, their capital at Camulodunum (Colchester) lay open,[14] and their chieftain Caratacus, realizing that all was lost, at least for the moment, withdrew into South Wales with those who preferred exile to the Roman yoke. Claudius was now able to take his place at the head of his army and entered the capital. There he made treaties with each submissive tribe individually, and gave Plautius his instructions for the completion of the conquest. He then departed to enjoy his triumph in Rome.

Although the main opposition had been removed there still remained some serious fighting for the Roman Army. The Durotriges of Dorset and Somerset proved to be intransigent, and Vespasian was obliged to reduce a series of great hill-forts one by one. The most dramatic evidence for this phase has come from Maiden Castle, where in the war cemetery remains of the hastily buried warriors were found. All were battle casualties, and through the backbone of one there was still transfixed a Roman catapult bolt.[15] Elsewhere it seems likely that the army was able to move into its new positions without any serious hostility. There were no great natural barriers across England along which to establish a frontier, but at least the Bristol Channel and lower Severn were a useful start. To the north-west ran the Cotswolds, a fine limestone escarpment which continues, but to a reduced extent, into Northampton-shire and Leicestershire, then rises up sharply once more to form the Lincoln Edge. Beyond this limestone belt are the Triassic claylands through which the rivers Avon and Trent have cut their way. In contrast to the lightly wooded limestone area, the clays supported thick forests with dense undergrowth, and to an observer standing on the northern edge of the Cots-wolds this mass of verdure would stretch as far as the eye could see, merging on the horizon into the midland plateau.[16] This was sufficient to impress the Roman governor, and it marked a convenient line on which his frontier could be established, when the further advantages of the Humber and lower Trent in the north and the Exe on the south coast are also considered. This decision was of the greatest importance to the future of the Roman province. A glance at its known sites and discoveries shows very clearly that the area of England to the south and east of this frontier is thick with towns, roads, and villas, very different from the sparsely occupied areas beyond, which with a few exceptions never escaped military control.[17]

If one can interpret from this evidence Roman ambitions for the new province, it seems that the policy of urbanization following in the wake of the army was to be confined to the south-east. Here was the greatest concentration of arable land and here, too, were the most civilized of the Britons, while for mineral wealth there were the rich silver deposits of the Mendips, the iron ores of the Weald and the limestone belt, and everywhere good timber for charcoal and building. Stone and clay were in abundance. Beyond to the north and west were the desolate forests and the upland areas with their tough hill folk.

Aulus Plautius consolidated along this line, and a strong argument can be advanced that here the Romans would have been content to stay. But the Britons 'beyond the pale' had other plans. The evidence for this frontier is not extensive, but the remarkable road, the Fosse Way, from Lincoln to the Devon coast, was recognized long ago by R. G. Collingwood as something exceptional, and he correctly deduced that it was part of a frontier system.[18] It appears, in fact, to be a medial line of communication in a fortified zone some thirty to forty miles in depth. Some of the forts have been found, and it seems that conditions varied considerably from one sector to another. The difficult terrain of the south-west forced the army to split into small holding garrisons, forming a tight network to keep down a hostile population. But elsewhere it is probable that a few large encampments were sufficient, provided there was a screen of forts in the forward area. Camulodunum remained the main military base, and it seems likely that the XXth Legion remained there to guard it and keep an eye on the Catuvellauni.

Plautius must have been well pleased with his work. He left to his successor a reasonably peaceful province held in strength, and part at least eager to embrace the new delights of Mediterranean living. But when his successor Ostorius Scapula arrived he found the province in a state of near chaos. The instigator of a new wave of open hostility was Caratacus, who had craftily waited for the winter season and the change of governors. He must have worked on the tribes of South Wales effectively with stories of atrocities and even worse, wholesale slavery. Led by the British prince, the Silures had crossed the Severn, and penetrating deep inside the Roman lines, had spread havoc far and wide. It was a difficult situation for the new governor, but rousing his army from their winter quarters he chased the tribesmen back across the Severn. He gave thought to the next moves. He could hardly allow the enemy freedom of action, for while Caratacus lived and fought, hope might surge in every British heart uncommitted to Roman ways. Ostorius realized at once that the Fosse frontier so carefully planned by Plautius was now outdated, since it gave the British too much room for manoeuvre; they could move along the forest trails and fall unheralded on almost any part of the line. The Roman Army was forced to move forward before their position was properly consolidated. In the south-west they were still hard pressed, while many of the tribes in the conquered parts were of uncertain allegiance and watched and waited for any opportunity. Nor did Scapula know how the Brigantes of the north might react. He could hardly afford to weaken the frontier, and he badly needed his strategic reserves in the Camulodunum base. The troops thus moved into the forward area could be replaced to some extent by veterans by the formation of a *colonia*. But this had its inherent dangers, as it entailed large-scale land appropriation. His next move seems almost one of desperation, for he resolved to disarm all the tribes. What precisely this meant it is difficult to say. Its value is doubtful, since swords and spears could have been rapidly mass-produced by the local blacksmiths. He may have made it into an act of sheer terrorism to overawe the tribes and keep them quiet while his army was in the field. His mistake was to include in this order the client-

kingdom of the Iceni. These proud and independent people
would have regarded themselves as immune from such a savage
enactment involving the invasion of privacy by thorough
search of homes and persons. There was a minor revolt, and as
most of the troops had by now been moved forward, it had to
be put down by a dismounted cavalry regiment. An interesting
fact emerges from the report by Tacitus, that the tribe was
copying Roman military defences in the building of turf
ramparts. By his act of ignoring the privileged position of the
Iceni, Scapula securely planted the seeds of discontent which
brought such a prodigious harvest later.

But the commander's thoughts were far away, wrestling
with the problem of Caratacus and the *terra incognita* which lay
before his army. The Roman method was a simple one, that of
seeking out the enemy and destroying him. How this was to be
accomplished quickly and easily was another matter. To make
a thorough sweep through this difficult tangled country of
forests and hills would take too long. More rapid success could
be achieved by encirclement; we must imagine the army
moving forward in a series of heavily armoured probes, feeling
their way along the easy routes. The fleet would be exploring the
south coast of Wales, looking for the best inlets and landing-
places. Another probe may have found the Wye Valley.
Another, we know, was feeling its way along the foothills as far
north as Flintshire, learning the geography of the Welsh
Marches and looking for the routes into central Wales.

This grim remorseless approach was viewed by Caratacus
with serious concern. If he waited in the Black Mountains he
could be easily surrounded and be forced to battle without hope
of extracting himself or his forces. He decided therefore to move
his standard north and oppose the Romans at a place of his
own choice, where he could reduce as much as possible the
effectiveness of the Roman arms. At the same time he could
rally more of the British tribes and swell his force. Many are
the claimants for the site of this celebrated battle, but most of
them fail if the description Tacitus gives has any reliability.
One of the important factors was the river before which the
legion hesitated. This could only be the Wye, Severn, or Dee.
It was most probably the Severn, and the site somewhere in the

difficult foothills beyond Welshpool. The British plan was to force the Romans to attack on a difficult and narrow front and restrict their use of cavalry. It was a grim battle, but the superior equipment and training of the Roman legions won the day. They hacked their way to the summit, to find that Caratacus and many of his levies had melted away. It was a victory for Scapula, but not a decisive one, and he was far away from his base. In his impotent fury he swore to annihilate the whole tribe of the Silures, but it might have been wiser to withdraw to the Severn and establish a strong frontier along its eastern bank.

At least the problem of Caratacus was to be solved for the Romans. He had fled north to Cartimandua, whom Claudius had established as queen over this vast confederacy of tribes. But her very position was dependent on the Roman will, and she could but hand over the British prince in chains. He was sent to Rome, upbraided the Emperor himself, and received a position of honoured captivity. Ostorius Scapula was now a sick man and his mind overwrought by his illness and by anxiety. He desperately attempted to get at grips with the enemy, but the Silures, hardened in defeat, adopted more resourceful methods. Using the woods and hills as cover, they carried out a relentless guerilla warfare on the harassed units who were trying to establish their forts in difficult terrain west of the Severn. Every move was watched and any small detachments on patrol liable to be surrounded and cut to pieces. Scapula was fighting a phantom army he could not bring to bay. It faded away as he approached, only to steal silently round his back, picking at stragglers and supply columns. Overburdened with his difficulties, the governor succumbed to his illness and died. The Silures had scored a notable victory.

There is a hint from Tacitus that the tribe had by bribes tempted others to join in their successful campaigns, and it is possible that after the death of Scapula the situation had become very serious for the Roman Army, and that a legion had been beaten in the field. Such was the position which faced the new governor Didius Gallus, who was dismissed by Tacitus as being of 'impressive seniority but incapacitated by age', for he had been consul as early as A.D. 36. He managed, however, to stop further serious trouble and even push forward at some unspecified point. During his lengthy governorship (A.D. 52–58) he faced difficulties with Brigantia. Cartimandua had divorced her husband Venutius and there was a civil war which was put down with the dispatch of a legion. During this period Claudius died. His successor was the young Nero, but in the early part of his reign Imperial affairs were in the hands of Burrus and Seneca. It may have been during this period that the evacuation of Britain was seriously considered. But in A.D. 57 hesitations and doubts were resolved. New decisions involved the army in forward movements at the two ends of the Empire, Corbulo in Armenia and a new governor, Veranius, in Britain. Here perhaps we see Nero himself taking a hand in affairs and spurning the cautious policy of his advisers.

The new governor of Britain, Quintus Veranius, has suffered much at the hands of historians. Tacitus has given us two facts, that Veranius died within a year of his coming to Britain and that in his will he had said that given two more years he would have conquered the rest of Britain. He is thus seen as vain and boastful, but added to this unfortunate picture he has also been considered aged. Professor E. Birley has shown,[19] however, that Veranius was, in fact, not older than 46 when he died, and that his career, which is well documented, proves that in spite of lowly ancestry he was an outstanding personality who had risen rapidly in Imperial service and must have been one of the most able commanders available at the time. Moreover, the terms of his will may have meant no more than confidence that he could complete his mission within the space of his governorship.

Ostorius and Didius Gallus were both operating under great difficulties imposed by the policy of a limited conquest dictated by Claudius. Otherwise they would have gone forward and dealt fully with the Silures and the rest of Wales. The result of this cautious policy was the creation of an unsatisfactory frontier with a continuous series of minor disasters. Veranius, active and of proved ability, was sent to initiate a change of strategy, and he was fully engaged in a determined advance which was continued by his successor. Although he had only a season's campaign, he must have been highly successful in dealing with the Silures, as Paulinus was able to advance into North Wales, and he could hardly have done this if the powerful tribe whose implacable hostility had caused so much trouble had been lurking untamed on his flank.

It remains to discuss the military situation in Britain and the disposition of troops at the outset of the governorship of Paulinus. Apart from a handful of troops acting as guards, messengers, and orderlies in the pacified areas of the province, the whole army was in the frontier zone. By now it was an area difficult of definition. The old line of Plautius must still have been held in part. The northern arm from High Cross or Leicester was still anchored to the Trent and Humber, and its command base, Lincoln, the headquarters of the IXth Legion. A cavalry regiment left its trace at Crococalana (Brough) with the decorated cheek-piece of a parade helmet now in Newark Museum. Ad Pontem, a fort at Thorpe-by-Newark, has been revealed by a crop-mark. There was a unit at Margidunum, but its actual fort is yet to be found. At Leicester there is the famous tile fragment bearing the imprint of the VIIIth Legion, but it is doubtful if a detachment which presumably came over in A.D. 43 would still be in Britain.[20] In a forward position was the fort at Broxtowe, Nottingham, now completely obliterated by a modern housing estate. In the rear the Great Casterton fort in Rutland appears still to be occupied although reduced in size. This part of the line must have been held in strength for fear of trouble from the north.

In the south-west also there may well have been some units still pinned down in their old forts, but by now perhaps thinned out as the Durotriges had been gradually subdued. Command headquarters may have been the legionary fortress at Gloucester. First established by Scapula on the Kingsholm site, now covered by modern housing, it may first have been occupied by the XXth, brought up from Colchester to plug the gap in those early hectic years against Caratacus. As the front moved forward and the south-west came slowly under control the XXth could have been withdrawn and replaced by the IInd *Augusta*, but the precise date remains in doubt.

In the Midland triangle there are several forts which show that, beyond the Fosse Way in this central area, the whole territory was under military control. The main line of advance and communication was the road known later as Watling Street and today as A5. Here is the genesis of the great London-Holyhead road. Already Scapula had carried it up to the Severn at Viroconium (Wroxeter) near Shrewsbury. Here at an early stage in these campaigns, probably as a base for the drive against Caratacus, the XIVth Legion had built its fortress. This site now seems to be buried ten or twelve feet below the later Roman town, but tombstones, early coins, pottery, and much

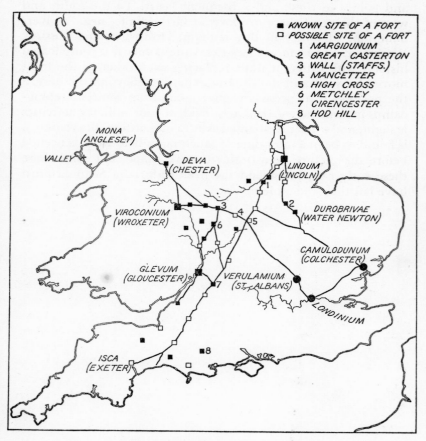

Fig. 3. The Roman Frontier Zone.

military equipment bear witness to its presence. We still have to account for the XXth Legion, and so far no satisfactory base for it has been suggested. As Paulinus took this legion with him to Anglesey we can presume that it must have been stationed somewhere between Wroxeter and Lincoln. A tempting site is Little Chester near Derby, but there is a small auxiliary fort here and no evidence so far of anything larger.[21] Along Watling Street itself there is growing evidence of much military activity, but it is difficult to separate and interpret the many comings and goings in these and subsequent years. To the south and west of this road there are forts at Greensforge, near Wolverhampton, Metchley in Birmingham, Droitwich, and possibly Worcester. But in most cases excavations reveal a complicated history, with different units replacing each other as the front moved forward and the situation changed. Beyond the Severn the position is at present vague; apart from some marching-camps in the Craven Arms area evidence for military activities is slight, and when investigated as at Leintwardine (Bravonium), is found to be of a later date.[22] Much more field work is needed before the picture here begins to take shape, but somewhere these early campaigns and the frontier forts of Scapula must have left their indelible marks.

3

BACKGROUND TO REBELLION

THE ROOTS OF THE GREAT REBELLION go back to the settlement imposed by Claudius after the defeat of the Belgae and the capture of Camulodunum. Both Tacitus and Suetonius give a short account of this settlement, and a contemporary record is to be found in the inscription from the arch of Claudius (now in the courtyard of the Conservatori Museum at Rome) and in the associated inscription from the arch at Cyzicus.[1] The first records that it was dedicated to Claudius by the Senate and People of Rome 'because he received the surrender of eleven kings of Britain, defeated without any loss, and because he was the first to bring barbarian peoples across the Ocean under the sway of the Roman people'.

Of the eleven kings it may be said that no British XI is harder to pick, but it included all those who made their surrender to Claudius, whether peacefully or after defeat, and shows that the invasion of Britain was accompanied or preceded by a carefully planned diplomatic offensive. Among those who went peaceably was certainly a ruler of the Iceni, whether Prasutagus or another, Cogidubnus, king of the Regni in Sussex, and perhaps Cartimandua or another ruler of the Brigantes in the north. It is easy to see the attractions of such a course for the Iceni. For more than forty years they had watched with alarm the growth of the Belgic kingdom into the most formidable power in Britain, to which a Roman observer could give the ominous title of *regnum Britanniae*.[2] Isolated in their corner of East Anglia, the Iceni could scarcely have hoped to remain independent for long. The Roman invasion altered the whole political position in Britain, but for the time being the Iceni and others remained frozen in their old attitudes. Hatred of the Belgae was more potent than fear of those who had struck them down. So their ruler went to Camulodunum to receive the status of client-king, as many another had done on all the frontiers of the Roman world.

Speaking of Cogidubnus's action at this time, Tacitus adds the tart comment that it was an old and long-established custom of the Roman people to employ even kings as the instruments of slavery. Old it certainly was, for the first instance of such a relationship was that established with King Hiero of Syracuse in the First Punic War, three hundred years earlier. It was employed lavishly in Republican times, especially on the eastern frontiers. Pompey's settlement of the east, which left a belt of client-kingdoms as a glacis against Parthia, shows the military and diplomatic aspects of the system fully deployed. On the African frontier, too, in Numidia and Mauretania, client-kingdoms played a valuable role by enabling Rome to exercise remote control over the desert peoples beyond the frontiers of the Roman provinces. In Judaea the complicated history of the Herods extended from 40 B.C. to the end of the first century A.D. Augustus brought the two largest Asian kingdoms, Galatia and Cappadocia, into the provincial system; by the time of the Flavians there were none left in Asia Minor. Under Gaius and Claudius the provincial system was extended to cover the whole North African coast. But there was still a part for client-kings on the northern frontiers, among the petty rulers of Alpine and Caucasian lands, as well as the more powerful communities like those of Marcomanni and of Thrace, which became a province in 46. North of the Black Sea the Bosporan kingdom remained on friendly terms with Rome, without being absorbed, for more than two hundred and fifty years.[3] In the time of Augustus it threw up a woman ruler, Queen Dynamis, whose character was very like that of Boudicca, though she met with better fortune in her dealings with Rome. It is, of course, impossible to deduce a set of principles for the treatment of client-kingdoms. Rome did not work that way. Each relationship was *ad hoc*; certain features are common enough to speak of a general pattern. First, the relationship was between Rome and the

individual ruler, not the kingdom. On his death or removal—
and she could remove him at will—Rome was free to consider
the position *de novo*. A successor, if appointed, was usually from
the Royal house. Some client-kings paid tribute, or made
voluntary contributions to Rome. All were liable to be called
upon to furnish troops and supplies; Galatia and Thrace were
notable recruiting-grounds for the Roman Army. On their side
the client-kings had the likelihood, though not the guarantee,
of Roman support against outside enemies or civil disorder.
Thus Cartimandua in Britain received Roman help against her
husband Venutius. Their dealings with powers other than Rome
were strictly controlled. When Herod Agrippa was rash enough
to organize a conference of neighbouring kings in 43, it was
abruptly broken up by the governor of Syria. Above all, by the
time of Claudius the whole trend was to make such arrangements shortlived; 'vassal status was by nature transitional, and,
as a rule, it was destined to lead ultimately to absorption'.[4] The
three British client-kings were, after all, among the smaller fry,
and to them this rule was applied without exception. None
could have been more loyal, none could have received more
marks of favour, than Cogidubnus. His own territory was increased, certain other tribes were placed under his rule, he
was granted Roman citizenship and the unique title of '*rex et
legatus Augusti in Britannia*'.[5] He remained faithful to Rome
throughout a reign of more than forty years. None the less,
on his death his kingdom was absorbed into the province. Small
wonder that the more unruly Iceni and Brigantes were to be
deprived of their independence when the opportunity came.

But these disadvantages lay in the future. In the years immediately after 43, the Iceni must have seen cause to congratu-
late themselves as their hostile neighbours were brought firmly
under Roman control and the province extended to the Severn
and the Trent. The disarming of the tribe by Ostorius Scapula
and the rebellion it provoked have already been described.
They came as a sharp reminder to the Iceni of what their
'independence' really amounted to, and no doubt left some
grievances. But these were at least assuaged by the prosperity
of the years 48–59, and we hear of no further troubles until the
death of Prasutagus.

Shortly after the first rebellion of the Iceni, in the winter of 48–49, came an event of grim portent for the Trinovantes, the founding of a powerful military colony at Camulodunum. Tacitus gives a succinct account of its purpose: 'to act as a support against the rebels, and to instruct the allies in the duties enjoined by the laws'.[6] Ostorius intended to move the legions forward to the Severn to come to grips with Caratacus. A force of veterans would be a substitute for a legionary garrison: it could keep an eye on the Iceni and put down another rising. Such military colonies had been a favourite device of Augustus in backward provinces, like Pisidia in the east and Lusitania in the west. Claudius founded some fifteen colonies, including, in the western provinces, two in Gaul, four in Mauretania, two in Germany, and one in Britain.[7] Cologne (Colonia Claudia ara Agrippinensis), founded in 51, offers some parallels with the history of Colchester, of which more will be said. None of these western colonies was on a wholly new site. In selecting Cunobelinus's old capital Claudius was making a conscious choice of the most suitable centre for the Romanization of the province. This is what is covered by Tacitus in the phrase about 'instructing the allies in the duties enjoined by the laws'. The new colony stood for that urban civilization which was the mark of Roman culture, and was the seat of the cult of Claudius which was to be the focus of provincial loyalties. Here would rise the great octastyle classical temple with the altar in front —an architectural scheme unusual in the provinces, which has been compared with the altar and temple of Divus Julius in the Roman Forum. This temple was the especial object of hatred to Boudicca and her followers; its *podium*, still surviving in the vaults of Colchester Castle, is a reminder of the grim scenes enacted in it. Besides the temple, Tacitus speaks of a theatre and a senate house. Colchester was a showpiece of cultural amenities. Amenity, not use, Tacitus notes, was then the keynote of official policy; the new colony was not provided with defences. It is clear, too, that from the first it had British inhabitants, whether survivors from the capital of Cunobelinus or immigrants from other parts of the province. But the veterans who formed the main element in the population stood for the less amiable side of Roman imperialism. From the *Eclogues* of

44

Virgil we see how selfish and arrogant these ex-soldiers could
be, even on Italian soil.[8] In a conquered province, and in a
district which had been the heart of resistance to Rome, there
was little to restrain their worst instincts. Their grants of land,
taken from the confiscated estates of the royal house of the Belgae,
do not seem to have been done on any regular system of cen-
turiation, but left to individual enterprise. 'They kept driving
the Britons off their lands,' says Tacitus, 'calling them prisoners
and slaves', as indeed, according to Roman law, they were. It
was settler politics at its worst, and in ten years it had driven
the Trinovantes to fury and a longing for revenge.

  Although the seeds of future trouble had been planted among
the Trinovantes and the Iceni, official propaganda could paint
a rosy picture of success in Britain up to the time of the surrender
of Caratacus in A.D. 51. A Roman expedition, well officered
and brilliantly led, had crossed the Channel in 43 to shatter
barriers both geographical and psychological. The formidable
power of the Belgae was quickly overthrown: the resistance of
most other *civitates* was shortlived, though sharp in the south-
west. Only in Wales, under Caratacus, was resistance prolonged.
When at length that prince was overcome, there was a notable
display of imperial *clementia* to a gallant adversary. The recklessness of the invasions of Caesar, the fiasco of Gaius, were not
repeated. There had been a break with the inertia of Tiberius.
The bounds of Empire had been extended to the western limits
of the known world, and the sacred *pomoerium* of Rome enlarged
by an Emperor whose piety had once again placed her in the
right relationship with the gods.

  But the last years of Claudius's reign saw this picture change
for the worse. We saw in an earlier chapter how the capture of
Caratacus had not solved the problem of Wales, for the Silures
were incorrigible, keeping up relentless pressure along the line
of the lower Severn. His successor, Didius Gallus, could do no
more than hold the position in the west. By 55 he was forced to
intervene in the north to support Cartimandua in a civil war
which had broken out among the Brigantes. In the early years
of Nero, Britain must have been something of a running sore, a
constant drain on troops and money without adequate returns.
Suetonius says that Nero once contemplated withdrawal from

Britain, and this period (54–57), as Birley has shown, is the context into which the proposal best fits.[9] It would have accorded with that imitation of Augustus which marked the policy of Nero, for the conquest of Britain was a major departure from Augustus's injunction against enlarging the Empire. But a certain *pietas* was due to Claudius by his successor and murderer. By 57 the decision had been taken to maintain the province and carry through the conquest of Wales. With the hour came the man. Q. Veranius had been early marked out for high command, and as governor of Lycia and Pamphylia had made a name in mountain warfare. His appointment as governor of Britain in 57 marked the adoption of a new forward policy. But this must have involved other decisions, especially on finance. If the defence of the British provincials was proving much more expensive than estimated, it would not be unfair to ask them to pay for it. Although none of the authorities mention it, it would not be surprising if there were a general revision of provincial taxes about this time. It was customary in the provinces to hold a census every five years under the supervision of magistrates called *Quinquennales*. In Britain probably only Camulodunum, Verulamium and Londinium were sufficiently urbanized for such a measure, but in the first two a census would have been due in 57. Possibly a general provincial census was held at the same time; possibly, too—for all this is conjecture—Catus Decianus, the procurator who was so hated in the province at the time of Boudicca's rebellion, was first sent out to draw up and supervise a new scheme of taxation. Veranius died before much had been done. With the appointment of his successor Suetonius Paulinus, the stage was set for the tragedy of the Great Rebellion.

To speak of it thus is no empty phrase. The best account is in Tacitus, supreme among historians for his dramatic qualities. And Tacitus, like the Greek tragedians, did not care for many actors on the stage. Even if we do not accept his high figures for Boudicca's army, or for the slain in the three captured Roman cities, it is clear that the rebellion involved at least 100,000 people. Of these ten are known by name. On the British side two only, Prasutagus and his wife Boudicca; we do not know the names of their two daughters. On the Roman, Suetonius

Paulinus the governor; Catus Decianus the procurator, and his successor Julius Classicianus; Petilius Cerealis, commander of the IXth Legion at Lincoln; Poenius Postumus, camp prefect of the IInd Legion at Gloucester; Agricola, who was on Suetonius's staff as a young officer, and finally Polyclitus, the man in charge of the Commission of Inquiry after the rebellion. All these come from Tacitus; Dio does not add to the list. Archaeology has given us one other name, that of Inda Pacata, wife of Julius Classicianus. Such is the Dramatis Personae.

Prasutagus died in 59. We do not know when his reign began. It is often assumed that he was the king of the Iceni who surrendered to Claudius in 43, but there are arguments on both sides. On the one hand is Tacitus's reference to his long prosperity (*'longa opulentia clarus'*)—a phrase which would well describe the sixteen years at least which would have been his if he were the first client-king of the Iceni. The argument from coinage points the other way. No coins of Prasutagus are known, and if a client-king would lose the right to issue his own coinage the surrender was presumably made by 'Saemu', if he was the last king to have minted. The rebellion of 47 must obviously have a bearing on this question, but it is hard to assess. It is surprising to find the client-kingship continued at all after a rising which also involved tribes from the Roman province. But continued it was, and it is tempting to suppose that Prasutagus was put in as a Roman nominee after the rebellion. If so, his long prosperity would have lasted no more than twelve years; even thus, Tacitus's phrase may be justified. If the rebellion was little more than the anti-Roman faction getting the upper hand for a while, then Ostorius might have allowed Prasutagus to remain on the throne, since his own hands were tied by more urgent business in Wales. So long as the evidence is so scanty the question would seem to be insoluble. What, then, of the renowned wealth of Prasutagus? So far, archaeology has not revealed much trace of it. We do not know where the Royal seat was. Perhaps near Thetford? Caistor seems to be Flavian at the earliest, and there is not much evidence of Romanisation on Icenian territory before that date, although a recent discovery at Lakenheath suggests trade on a considerable scale.[10] The territory has few mineral resources, apart from some iron in north-west Norfolk which might have been worked. Agriculture, then, would seem the most likely source of Prasutagus' wealth, not the corn of modern Norfolk farming, but sheep and cattle, for which both the greensand and the Fen margin would provide a good pasture. The date of his marriage to Boudicca is fixed within limits by the fate of his two daughters. In 59 these girls were too young to play any political part in the rebellion, but old enough to be raped. To ask how old that is may be thought to treat history as an art rather than a science. But one is perhaps entitled to hope that the younger girl was at least twelve, even fourteen; her sister must have been at least a year older. In other words, the marriage of Prasutagus and Boudicca cannot have been later than 45 and may have been earlier than 43.

Prasutagus is a shadowy figure compared with his wife. In both Tacitus and Dio, Boudicca stands out clearly, a passionate and powerful figure to be set beside those other great barbarians whom we know through the eyes of their Roman enemies —Arminius, Caratacus, and even Vercingetorix. Yet we know curiously few facts about her. Even her status among the Iceni is in doubt. It has been suggested that she was the Queen-regnant, like Cartimandua among the Brigantes, and that Prasutagus became her husband as Roman nominee to bring the Iceni to heel after the rebellion. But, if the date for the marriage suggested above is right, it is possible that she was not of Icenian origin at all, for in the ruling dynasty of a Celtic tribe outside marriages were common. Tacitus's phrase 'a woman of the Royal house' seems carefully chosen to suggest that, in the Roman view, she had no claim to the succession after her husband's death. When he adds that 'they do not distinguish between the sexes in positions of authority', he is referring to her position as war-leader of the British confederacy —of which more later—and not to sovereignty of the Iceni. But it seems clear that her people regarded her as their natural leader after her husband's death, and that their neighbours were willing to follow her into the fearful hazards of an anti-Roman rising.

There are more facts to go on about Suetonius Paulinus.[11] He was one of the group of brilliant generals—Aulus Plautius,

Hosidius Geta, Vespasian, Corbulo—selected for high command at the beginning of Claudius's reign. His achievement stands out even in that company. As governor of Mauretania (41–42) he had led the first Roman army to cross the High Atlas, and crushed opposition by depriving the mountain peoples of their supplies in the oases to the south. The French and Spanish generals who fought Abd-el-Krim in these mountains could best appreciate what this means. Returning to Rome in 43, he was rewarded with the *triumphalia ornamenta* and the consulship, but does not seem to have received another command until he was sent to Britain in 58 to take up the task which Veranius had left unfinished. It is not fanciful to suggest that he was sent for as a specialist in mountain warfare, for the Welsh mountains and the granary of Anglesey behind them presented the same problems as the High Atlas and the Saharan oases. The new forward policy of Nero, in the east and the west, was followed with great popular expectation which looked to Suetonius Paulinus to rival in Britain the feats of Corbulo in Armenia. He must have been a man of above sixty[12] when he arrived in Britain to take up this mission.

Unfortunately for the province, Suetonius seems to have conceived his task almost wholly in military terms. In any case, the Augustan system of provincial administration made a sharp division between the powers of the *legatus* or governor and those of the *procurator* or finance officer, who was concerned with all issues affecting the imperial treasury. This separation of powers was thought to be in the interests of good government, and it is true that the general level of provincial administration was markedly higher under the Empire than under the Republic. Not that the two officials were in watertight compartments; it was the duty of the *legatus* to check any excess of the *procurator* that might be bad for the morale of the province, while the *procurator* could interfere if the governor's policy threatened its economic viability. But the possibilities of collusion were there, although the social gap between the legate, usually of aristocratic origin, and the *procurator*, drawn from the *equites* or business class, meant that their relations were often unfriendly. Such collusion usually took the form of an agreement to live and let live—or what Tacitus, in another context, calls a '*mutuam dissimulationem mali*'. In such cases the unhappy provincials might well feel, as they did under Suetonius Paulinus, that 'once they had one king at a time on their backs, now they had two, of whom the *legatus* tyrannized over their persons and the *procurator* over their possessions'. Provincial taxation was not, at this period, unduly burdensome in itself.[13] Its most important items were the land-tax (*tributum soli*), levied on all landowners, and property-tax (*tributum capitis*). Besides these there were customs-dues (*portoria*) and requisitions of various kinds, the most important being that of corn (*annona*). In Britain, a corn-growing country, and with an exceptionally large garrison of not less than 50,000 men, this last item must have been onerous. A famous passage of Tacitus (*Agricola*, 19, 4) details a number of rackets which had grown up in the collection of the *annona*; although they belong to a date twenty years later than Boudicca's rebellion, it is unlikely that they were new inventions. But these were the responsibility of the army officials who collected the *annona* on behalf of the governor. In 59 and 60 it was the *procurator*, Catus Decianus, who was the source of trouble. All we know of him puts him in a very bad light—a Verres born out of his time. The British taxpayers, as Tacitus expressly notes, were a patient body of men, provided there was no unfairness, but that they would not stand.[14] Unfairness they seem to have got in plenty from Catus Decianus, to judge from the reactions, though we only see him in operation in his dealings with the Iceni. But there were other hands reaching for the British taxpayer's windpipe besides those of the officials. The expenses of Romanization were heavy for communities and individuals, and in every newly won province there were Roman moneylenders ready to make it available on hire-purchase terms. The letters of Cicero about his term as governor of Cilicia throw a lurid light on the way in which these private creditors could use the machinery of provincial administration to put pressure on provincial debtors. That was, of course, in the bad old days of the Republic, but it is unlikely that such practices were wholly extinct under the Empire. At any rate, it is clear that in 59 and 60 the private moneylenders operating in Britain felt they were overextended and began to call in their loans. A new system of provincial taxation, or the launching of new military operations, would be cause enough, severally or jointly, to promote such action. If, as Dio says, Seneca was the largest operator, having no less than 40 million sesterces out on loan in Britain, then there would have been a scandalous alignment of government policy and private interest. But the Seneca story is found only in Dio, not in Tacitus, and Syme has recently shown good reasons for doubting it.[15] But Seneca or not, there was a financial panic in Britain, and a harsh and unprincipled *procurator*. Prasutagus had chosen a bad moment to die.

It is a pity that a discrepancy between Tacitus and Dio leaves in doubt the exact circumstances at the time of his death. That he foresaw difficulties is certain from what Tacitus says about the terms of his will, which left the Emperor co-heir with his two daughters 'in the belief that this mark of attention would result in the kingdom and his household escaping harm'.[16] It is to be noted that there is no suggestion that the client-kingship was to be perpetuated. What Prasutagus seems to have hoped was to secure for his people a safe transition to incorporation within the province—always a delicate operation, since they would for the first time come fully under the control of the Roman tax officers. His precautions were vain, in the event, and the Iceni underwent a most brutal experience. Dio provides a reason for this by his statement that Catus Decianus was treating as recoverable certain moneys that Claudius had given to 'their leaders';[17] whether the leaders of the Iceni alone, or whether other tribes were included, is not certain. But the implication is clear. What the Britons had taken as a grant was now being called a loan, and, no doubt, with arrears of interest included. Although Dio links this with the story of a loan from Seneca, which we have seen reason to doubt, there is no need to discard this part of his account as well. For it would go far to explain Prasutagus's will and the subsequent action of Catus Decianus. Prasutagus seems to have regarded his legacy to Nero as fully covering his obligations to Rome. Catus Decianus ruled otherwise. The whole country was treated as though it had been given to Rome; the estates of the kinsmen of the Royal house were alienated and they themselves sold into slavery. Boudicca herself was flogged and the two princesses raped. These atrocities have stirred patriotic indignation in many a schoolboy's breast. But, granted that Decianus was a crook, and the centurions accompanying him were ruffians if they got out of hand, there must have been resistance to provoke them to such behaviour. And such resistance must have derived from Boudicca herself. Much of the blame must attach to Suetonius Paulinus, who was content to leave the handling of the Iceni to subordinate officials, because, in his own belief, he had other and bigger fish to fry. It was to prove a most costly mistake.

Above all, the problem of Wales had exercised Suetonius and his predecessor Veranius. Veranius had made some headway—perhaps a good deal—against the Silures in the south; Suetonius in two years' successful campaigning had consolidated these gains and added to them, most probably in central and eastern Wales, the later principality of Powys. But in the north-west, always the stronghold of Welsh independence, a formidable native power still confronted him. The mountains of Snowdon gave them a natural stronghold, and behind these was the great granary of Mona or Anglesey, 'thickly populated, and a safe retreat for fugitives' in the words of Tacitus. The 'fugitives' were not merely those of Caratacus's followers still in arms, but, we may be sure, anti-Roman elements from all the tribes of Britain. For in Mona was the headquarters of Druidism, the rallying-point, in Britain as in Gaul, of all the forces of Celtic nationalism.

It is natural to feel a certain hesitation on the subject of the Druids. Eighteenth-century antiquarianism, and too much later bogus mysticism, have invested it with an air of the spurious and the absurd. But to the Roman administration in Gaul and Britain that powerful priesthood was a grim reality for more than a hundred years. The Druids had been behind both the rising of Vercingetorix against Caesar and the rebellion of Florus and Sacrovir in A.D. 21. Augustus had forbidden the cult to Roman citizens; Tiberius drove Druid priests out of Gaul; Claudius attempted to stamp out the cult in that province.[18] None the less, it survived to proclaim, amid the troubles of the year A.D. 69, that the Empire of the world was passing from Rome to the peoples of the north.[19] In Britain, its role was the same, its influence even stronger. The influence of the Druids may well have accounted for the acceptance of Caratacus as their war-leader by the tribes of Wales. It must have reached into every British state, within and without the Roman province, linking together anti-Roman parties, fanning discontent and sedition. Archaeologically, it is dramatically attested by the famous hoard from Llyn Cerrig Bach, now in the National Museum of Wales, and to be discussed in a later chapter. The final reduction of the Silures could await its turn; this was the power Suetonius meant to crush in its stronghold beyond the mountains of Eryri. Success would not only be a deadly blow at Celtic nationalism, but would give Rome a valuable prize in the shape of the copper of Parys Mountain, one of the richest deposits of that metal in north-western Europe.

While Suetonius was moving troops up to the north-west frontier, events of which he had little knowledge were mounting rapidly to a climax deep in his rear. He had failed disastrously to keep his finger on the pulse of the province, or to gauge the mounting tide of resentment for which his absence in Wales provided such an opportunity. As a result, when the great rebellion broke out, all his forces were pointed the wrong way. The Britons put his absence to good use. First came secret conferences, at which, in Tacitus's phrase, 'they compared their grievances, and inflamed each other by the constructions they put upon them'. The grievances of the Iceni were, of course, the outrages they had suffered at the hands of Catus Decianus, those of the Trinovantes the insolent behaviour of the veterans at Colchester, and, common to all, the burdens of Roman taxation, the harshness of the moneylenders, and the expenses of maintaining the cult of Claudius at Colchester. To add to these grievances of their own there was the powerful stimulant of anger at the Roman attack on the headquarters of the Druidic religion, the vital element in the native Celtic culture. It can hardly be a coincidence that there was such a widespread rebellion at precisely this juncture. Though neither Tacitus nor Dio mention it, the political influence of the Druids must have been used to urge the other *civitates* to join Boudicca. Next, when a decision to join forces in a rising had been reached, a council of chiefs must have met to appoint a war-leader, agree on the contributions to be made by each tribe, and decide the general strategy of the campaign. Finally, there would have been a hosting of all the tribes; and Rome would be confronted by what she had most to fear on any of the northern frontiers of the Empire, a confederacy of barbarian peoples. For obvious reasons, these last two events must have taken place on Icenian soil. To this prelude to the rebellion, which must have occupied several months, Tacitus devotes a single chapter of the *Agricola*, and a few lines of the account in the *Annals*. He does not distinguish its phases, being interested only in a general picture of the motives that prompted the British rising. These, characteristically, are expounded in a reported speech in *oratio obliqua*. Characteristically, too, Dio expands the arguments found in Tacitus into a forcible-feeble speech of great length, which he puts into the mouth of Boudicca on the occasion of the hosting, adding to his account certain details which must come from other sources. It cannot be said that Dio contributes much to our understanding of the British case. But one of his details is vivid and valuable—the description of Boudicca herself.

'She was huge of frame, terrifying of aspect, and with a harsh voice. A great mass of bright red hair fell to her knees: she wore a great twisted golden necklace, and a tunic of many colours, over which was a thick mantle, fastened by a brooch. Now she grasped a spear, to strike fear into all who watched her, and spoke as follows . . .'[20]

Unhappily, Dio's speech does not do her justice, but he has given us the most dramatic picture of a Celtic heroine in classical literature. Archaeologically, too, the torc and the fibula or cairngorm, are impeccable; the tunic of many colours may have been a tartan. One would like to know the source of the description. But we must look beyond Tacitus and Dio to what is known of northern society for a fuller understanding of Boudicca's position, of the workings of barbarian confederacy, and its potentialities. For this there is no lack of evidence. Caesar says a good deal about political conditions in the Gaul of his day; we can watch in the *Commentaries* the rise and fall of the great Gallic confederacies through the eyes of the man who had to deal with them in diplomacy and in the field. The most dangerous of them all, the rising under Vercingetorix, is particularly instructive.[21] The son of a great chieftain of the Arverni, Vercingetorix was by birth, education, and family tradition, the heir to all that was best in the native culture. But he also knew Rome and Roman military methods; the Arverni had held aloof from earlier anti-Roman movements, and Vercingetorix himself had served for six years in Caesar's camp. But in the late winter of 52 B.C. the harshness of Caesar's policy, the rapacity of Roman moneylenders and merchants, had brought all Gaul to the point of rebellion. Caesar's absence in Italy and the political troubles in which he was involved provided the opportunity. An anti-Roman rising was planned at the annual meeting of the council of the Gauls in the territory of the Carnutes, the headquarters of the Druidic cult, at which Vercingetorix was elected war-leader; after a short struggle to assert himself against the pro-Roman party amongst the Arverni, he stood at the head of a confederacy comprising nearly all the tribes of Gaul. Caesar comments on the energy and strictness with which he exercised his authority as war-leader. His position was confirmed when the structure of the confederacy was overhauled after the adhesion of the Aedui. Yet his powers were not unlimited. His general strategy had to be approved by a council of chiefs, and he did not always get his own way. Eloquence in council was as important as military skill to Vercingetorix; all depended on his personal authority and leadership. In the field he trained the Gauls in new tactics, including the techniques of siege warfare. In politics he stood above all intertribal jealousies for a conception of a free and independent Gaul which he believed could resist any power in the world. He was the embodiment of his country's cause, and when he surrendered after the disaster of Alesia it was lost. By contrast, the rising in Germany under Arminius succeeded in that it put an end, in effect, to Roman plans for the conquest of Germany. His victory over Varus in A.D. 9 was won as the leader of a confederacy of four tribes—Cherusci, Chatti, Marsi, and Bructeri. No barbarian leader can match his record of the massacre of Varus's three legions and effective opposition to Germanicus with his force of eight. It is interesting to find, in Tacitus's account of the prelude to rebellion, that the memory of Arminius's exploits encouraged the Britons to withstand Rome in their turn.[22] Nor was it necessary to look across the Channel. To oppose Caesar's second British expedition in 54 B.C. the tribes of Kent offered supreme command to Cassivellaunus, the great Belgic chieftain. Few of Caesar's opponents, native or Roman, came off so well. His switch to guerilla warfare after he had seen the folly of opposing Caesar in pitched battles was highly effective; even after the Romans had crossed the Thames and captured his capital at Wheathampstead, his authority was strong enough to induce his Kentish allies to attack Caesar's naval base. Both sides were ready for peace at the end of the summer, and if Caesar professed to be content with the campaign, the Britons on their side had solid grounds for satisfaction, for their efforts, in the event, won them nearly a hundred years of freedom.

Caratacus, too, after his defeat in the south-east, was able to organize resistance with far greater effect in Wales. As head of a confederacy of the tribes of Wales he won some notable success in eight years of struggle, and his movement became a focus for all anti-Roman forces in Britain, while his diplomacy was active among all the uncommitted tribes, especially the Brigantes in the north. It is pertinent, too, for us to recall the successful resistance, twenty years after Boudicca, to Agricola's invasion by the confederacy of all the Caledonian tribes under Calgacus. The description of the Caledonian host mustered for the battle of Mons Graupius prompts Tacitus (forgetting Boudicca and Caratacus) to the remark that 'at last the Britons had learned to repel common danger by common action, and by embassies and treaties had mobilized all the forces of their states'.[23] Their numbers, he says, amounted to not less than 30,000 fighting men. Though losses at the battle of Mons Graupius were heavy, their efforts were not in vain. For this was the supreme offensive of Rome in Caledonia; and at the end of it the Highland tribes retained the freedom for which they fought.

Boudicca's position, and what it might lead to, should by now be clear. How many British states took part in the confederacy we do not know. Tacitus says that it was a general rising, '*sumpsere universi bellum*', but there is no evidence that the peoples of Kent or Sussex took part, and *'universi'* may mean all who attended the council at which the rising was planned. To the Iceni and Trinovantes we may perhaps add the Coritani of the east Midlands, perhaps the Cornovii on their west, and the Durotriges of the modern Dorset, with partisans from the Catuvellauni, the Brigantes, and the Dobunni. And in every British tribe there would be those who would watch and wait, ready to join the rebellion if it made headway.

As we consider this phase of the rebellion certain questions arise to which there is no ready answer. Above all, why were the Britons able to go so far undetected, and why were the Roman authorities so negligent? The unreported hosting of so large an army seems hard to understand, even if we do not accept anything like Dio's figure of 120,000 men. The Iceni, no doubt, could muster their full force quickly; by isolating Camulodunum, the Trinovantes may have done the same. For the rest, we must imagine small bands slipping through the forests or across the fen to join the liberating army in the lands of the Iceni. Roman negligence is perhaps best ascribed to that overconfidence which so often besets colonial powers. A recent official report has severely criticized the Government of Kenya for their failure to grasp the true nature of the Mau Mau rising in its early stages. Above all, the Roman authorities seem to have counted too confidently on the loyalty of the provincials; that is why Tacitus speaks of a *'repentina defectio'*, a sudden breaking of allegiance. Moreover, the Romans seem to have had the fixed idea that the Britons were virtually incapable of forming confederations: *'singuli pugnant, universi vincuntur'*—one by one, that is the way—is the complacent statement of the *Agricola*, even after Caratacus and Boudicca! And again, fixed ideas as to the limitations of 'the natives' have brought disaster to many a colonial administration. So Suetonius may have thought that, if there was trouble during his absence in Wales, it would be confined to the Iceni, and could easily be contained by the forces available in the legionary base at Lincoln and the forts of the east Midlands. British propaganda, too, can probably take credit for keeping Roman eyes shut to the last minute. In the one instance where we can see it in action it seems to have been highly successful. At Camulodunum a double policy of playing on Roman fears and soothing Roman suspicions was followed by the British fifth column within the city. Within the theatre there were howlings in a foreign tongue, the statue of Victory (whether in the temple or some other public place) fell down and lay with its back turned as though surrendering to an enemy, keening women foretold disaster, a submerged apparition of the colony was seen in the waters of the Thames estuary, there were blood-red tides, leaving what looked like human corpses on the shore. All this was alarming—and good organization. But when the authorities of Camulodunum became apprehensive their fears were soothed by those Britons within the city who were privy to the plot. As a result, they never carried out an evacuation of the women and children, nor, until the very last moment, improvised any form of defence. So, through Roman negligence and their skill in exploiting it, the Britons won the initiative, and the first stages of the rebellion went forward according to plan.

Meanwhile, Suetonius's campaign in Wales had met with brilliant success. He ranks with Edward I as an invader of North Wales, having the same firm grip on the cardinal fact that no conquest can be permanent unless based on the control of the coast. Although we know few details of the Roman plans, they seem to follow a similar pattern. First a safe, secure base had to be found from which to make all preparations, and as the sea route was used, a harbour was necessary. By far the best harbour on this coast was at Chester on the Dee. It is difficult today as one stands on the medieval walls of this ancient city to appreciate its place as a port in Roman and later periods. When the Normans later built the weir to direct the waters into their corn mills they interfered with the scouring action of the tidal waters and from that day forward the river gradually silted up. In spite of various remedies Chester lost its valuable harbour to the upstart Liverpool, with its many natural disadvantages. Chester became a legionary base in about A.D. 75, but there is evidence of an earlier phase. In the north-eastern part of the fortress cremation burials have been found, in one case with a vessel of mid-first century date,[24] all clearly indicating the presence of a base prior to A.D. 75 and most likely to be that of Suetonius. The land route along the coast was not too difficult and the Degeangli of Flintshire had already been terrorized by Scapula.

The forces which Suetonius had available were the greater part of the two legions, the XIVth and XXth, with possible detachments from the others and about an equivalent number of auxiliaries. In addition he would have had the services of the fleet brought up from their nearest bases in the Bristol Channel. Altogether he probably mustered between 20,000 and 25,000 men. Tacitus says in the *Agricola* (14, 4) that he had two seasons in the field before the actual attack across the Menai Straits. This enabled him to establish his base at Chester, push his forces along the coastal route, and reduce any opposition to the south of Snowdonia. The route he might have taken would be the Severn and Tanat valleys across to Lake Bala, then either down to the sea at the Mawddach estuary, or across the hills towards the site of the fort at Tomen-y-Mur and the Portmadoc estuary. Two campaigns may well have been necessary to encircle the Snowdon massif and build the flat-bottomed boats at Chester ready for the crossing of the Menai Straits. Suetonius seems virtually to have completed the conquests of North Wales and little was left to his successors. With his experiences of mountain warfare in the Atlas, he was not likely to minimize the difficulties, and his approach work and consolidation was thorough. The leaders of the Druids watched these preparations for the attack with growing alarm. Ireland alone offered shelter, but from there hold over the British would be too remote to be effective. The Menai Straits was to be their last ditch. Only by their strong political influence could disaster be avoided. It seemed unlikely that the Roman Army could be diverted from its target or lured into a trap. All now depended on the final throw. But the feverish machinations of the Druids came too late. Suetonius may have surprised them by his speed, for before they could act his army was drawn up along the Straits, and only their magic arts could save them now. Tacitus with his usual terseness sketches the scene as he may have heard it from the lips of Agricola himself. 'The enemy lined the shore in a dense armed mass. Among them were black-robed women with dishevelled hair like Furies, brandishing torches. Close by stood Druids, raising their hands to heaven and screaming dreadful curses. This weird spectacle awed the Roman soldiers into a kind of paralysis. . . .' But at the sound of their trumpets and the harsh words of command, discipline prevailed and they plunged forward, the infantry in their boats, the cavalry swimming with their horses. Soon it was all over, Druids, men, and women, swept under and butchered. The sacred groves were hacked down and the fires of fanaticism stamped out by hobnail boots.

But at this dramatic moment of victory a dispatch rider flung himself from his sweat-drenched horse and thrust into the hands of Suetonius his first intimation of disaster in the rear.

4

THE GREAT REBELLION: BRITISH WOLVES AND ROMAN FOXES

BEAUTIFULLY TIMED and vigorously pressed, the sudden out-break of the rebellion brought immediate success to the Britons. But the capture of Camulodunum was no Pearl Harbour, as Tacitus's narrative suggests. It is hard to disentangle the opening moves, and a discrepancy between the *Agricola* and the *Annals* does not help. But the settlers at Camulodunum had time to send to London for reinforcement; they could have built a rampart and palisade, and organized the evacuation of the women and children, though they neglected to do so. There was also time for the news of Boudicca's movements to reach the base of the IXth Legion at Lincoln, and for a rescue force to get under way. At least a week must be allowed for these events. If we accept the statement of the *Agricola*, that the attack on the *colonia* was preceded by the capture of Roman forts, a still longer period must be assumed. But, once the British force had closed in on Camulodunum, the end was swift. Catus Decianus had been unable—or unwilling—to spare more than 200 men from London. There was a small garrison in the *colonia*, and, of course, many of the veterans could still put up a fight. But they were hopelessly outnumbered, the town was without fortifications, and the only strongpoint was the temple of Claudius. Here they made their last stand, after the Britons had captured and fired the rest of the town. After two days of

61

desperate fighting, the defenders hoping against hope for the arrival of the force from Lincoln, it was stormed. The hated veterans could expect no mercy from the exploited Britons, and none was shown them. 'In the frenzy of victory the barbarians omitted no form of atrocity.' The 'seat of slavery' had been erased, and a prime objective of the rising attained.

A second success followed, more important as a feat of arms. The relief force which Petilius Cerialis took from Lincoln was a mixed body of as many men of the IXth Legion as could be spared, together with what auxiliary units could be picked up *en route*. He may have thus built up a task force of 5,000–6,000 men. Its most likely route would have been down the Ermine Street to Water Newton, thence by Godmanchester, Cambridge, and Horseheath. Somewhere along the Fen margins, perhaps between Water Newton and Godmanchester, it was met by a British force, and its infantry cut to pieces—probably in an ambush. Only the cavalry, with Petilius Cerialis at their head, managed to get back to Lincoln. A first reading of Tacitus suggests that this was the work of the British troops who had captured Camulodunum, but it is more likely that it was another British force, specially posted for this purpose. Whoever they were, these men had put out of action the only Roman force in eastern Britain capable of meeting Boudicca in the field. Colchester had gone. London and St. Albans were defenceless. There was hope only if Suetonius could move faster—and Boudicca slower—than anyone had a right to expect. At this point we are able to judge how the situation appeared to Catus Decianus. No one was better able to appraise it, and none had a higher position, as a personal target, on the British list. Deserting his post, the Roman *procurator* took ship and fled to the Continent. With him, in all probability, went his personal staff, depriving the province of any civil authority above the level of urban magistrates.

As for Suetonius, he could not have been worse placed to meet the disaster that now confronted him. He had with him in North Wales, 250 miles from London, more than half, perhaps as much as two-thirds, of the Roman troops in Britain. The IXth Legion at Lincoln was crippled and out of action. A few Roman forts might still be holding out in the areas overrun by Boudicca, but they could be no help to him, nor he to them. From the garrisons of the forts in the Trent-Severn gap, and the holding-force at Chester and Wroxeter, he could pick up some reinforcement, though probably not very much. But the picture was not all black. There was still the IInd *Augusta*, a legion with a fine fighting record. It had been with Vespasian in his drive to the south-west at the time of the Claudian conquest; later it had seen some hard fighting against the Silures. Its *legatus* was not with his unit, and the presumption is that he was commanding a detachment on active service in North Wales. But the bulk of the legion, perhaps 4,000 men, was at its southern base, under the command of a *praefectus castrorum*, Poenius Postumus, and if this was at Gloucester it lay only seventy miles—two days' march—from the line Suetonius must follow to London. The availability of this force must have played a major part in his strategy of pushing ahead with his cavalry, and leaving the infantry to make the best pace they could. Suetonius's plan would be to make for a rendezvous with Poenius Postumus and whatever other reinforcements could be mustered. A glance at the map will show three places where their forces might have been joined. One is Wall (Letocetum), near Lichfield, reached from Gloucester through Worcester, Droitwich, and Birmingham. Another, twenty-five miles closer to London, is at High Cross (Venonae), where the Fosse Way crosses the Watling Street. A third possibility is Towcester. No direct road is known between Gloucester and Towcester; but a rendezvous there would leave the IInd less distance to cover than the other two places, and nearer to London at the end of it. Against this, it should be said that no fort is known to have existed at Towcester. At one or another, Suetonius had counted on assembling a substantial force, both infantry and cavalry, which could be in London in another four days.

In his third year of campaigning, Suetonius would have a thorough grasp of military routes in North Wales. For his cavalry dash to the Midlands there would be the same choice that now confronts the motorist from Anglesey to London—the coastal route to Chester, or through the mountains to the Conway valley, then across the Denbigh moors to the Dee, the line of Telford's road. Imagination is stirred by the thought of the Roman cavalry threading through the wild mountains at the head of Nant Ffrancon on their desperate mission. Whichever way they took, no more than two days' hard riding would bring them to the Midland rendezvous. Here Suetonius was met by terrible news. The IInd Legion had failed him; Poenius Postumus had been unwilling to leave the defences of his fortress. 'Contrary to his military oath, he had disobeyed the commands of his general.' Such is Tacitus's unbending judgement, and, for such conduct, Poenius Postumus had, in the end, to pay with his life. At the bar of history he is known only for cowardice and suicide. He is perhaps entitled to ask us to view the situation through his eyes and at least to try to understand why he acted as he did. The legion—at Gloucester?—guarded the most dangerous frontier in the province. Where Cerialis at Lincoln had confronted rather doubtful allies in the Brigantes, the IInd Legion had for more than ten years been engaged with the most contumacious of all the Celtic peoples in Britain, the Silures. Earlier in the *Annals*, Tacitus stresses how they were by no means cowed at Caratacus's defeat, and his account of the fighting which followed along the line of the Severn makes it clear that the IInd Legion was barely able to hold its own. In one action (in 52?) a predecessor of Poenius as *praefectus castrorum* was killed, together with eight centurions. Nor, perhaps, were the Silures the only source of anxiety. The Durotriges had put up a stiff resistance to Vespasian's army at the time of the Claudian invasion, and anti-Roman feeling among them may still have been strong. They could have been very useful to the British cause by helping to contain the IInd at Gloucester, even if they did not join in the opening moves of the rebellion. To move the legion, he might have argued, would mean that the whole south-western frontier would be swept away. Moreover, the fate of the troops led by Cerialis to Camulodunum was a fearful warning of what might happen to Roman infantry trapped by British forces in overwhelming numbers—and we do not know whether Poenius Postumus had any cavalry to screen him. But there are other implications yet. Boudicca's forces could hardly have interrupted him between Gloucester and High Cross; a quick move from Gloucester should have eluded the Silures. It looks as though the Dobunni themselves must have joined the rebellion, or have been on the brink of it. As he hesitated between the clear duty of obeying his general's commands and the known hazards of doing so, Poenius must have felt himself in a dreadful trap. And here, perhaps—though we must not press this—his origins may have counted against him. As *praefectus castrorum*, he would be a man who had come up from the ranks, spent most of his life as a centurion, and had now reached the senior post open to him in the army. Such men were the backbone of the Roman Army, but they would lack the training of a legionary commander in the taking of big decisions. So Poenius Postumus, a man, it would seem, of ordinary competence caught in a situation far too big for him, weighed the odds and decided to stay where he was. Yet desperate odds can be faced and overcome by men with extraordinary resolution. Poenius Postumus did not have this quality—Suetonius did.

The situation Suetonius was now in called for resolution in full measure. He must have been strongly tempted to call off the march to London. To wait until the infantry came up from Wales would make him too late; to press on with the cavalry was to risk the fate of Cerialis's dash to Colchester. Tacitus is right to praise the *mira constantia* which induced him to hold on through the midst of the enemy—clearly the whole territory of the Catuvellauni, perhaps of the Coritani as well, was by now in rebel hands. The obvious route direct down Watling Street may well have been too dangerous. But, whatever the detour, he would almost certainly have reached London in little more than two days from High Cross or Wall. In the passage of Tacitus describing Suetonius's march London is mentioned for the first time. Less than twenty years old, it was already the busiest and most populous city of Britain, as it has been ever since. 'Not dignified by the name of a colony, but crowded with merchants and provisions' is Tacitus's description—a raw, booming town in a frontier province. 'What a city to sack!' old Blücher exclaimed as he rode through it after Waterloo: Boudicca's men thought of slaughter rather than loot. To Suetonius London was, as it has often been in its long history, a military objective of supreme importance. It was the hub of communications in Britain; here, if it could be held, reinforcements from the Continent could be disembarked within striking distance of the rebels. If it could be held—but that could only be determined on the spot. Suetonius approached London with his plans undecided. Again, he found the situation worse than he expected. Catus Decianus had fled overseas, and his staff with him: the city was undefended: there had been no time even to improvise a defence as at Colchester, nor was there any such reserve of fighting men as the veterans. Even if a long siege had been a military possibility, it is unlikely that he could have found provisions for so large a population. True, Cogidubnus and the friendly kingdom of the Regni were not far away, and he must at least have thought of an organized evacuation. But to get them all on the move would take time that could not be spared with the Britons closing in on London. He lacked the troops to cover an orderly movement; perhaps the Regni could not have fed the refugees if they had appeared. There was nothing for it but an agonizing reappraisal, the more harrowing because of the tears and entreaties of the Londoners, who at last saw what was impending—a disaster of a kind that Rome had not known for at least a century. Military disasters there had been. At Carrhae (55 B.C.) against the Parthians and in the Teutoberger Wald against Arminius (A.D. 9) Roman armies had been cut to pieces, but they were operating deep in enemy territory. In the grim days of the fearful Illyrian revolt under Augustus the Romans never lost their two great bases of Sirmium and Siscia. Under Tiberius, Tacfarinas had besieged the colony of Thubuscum, but (unlike Camulodunum) it had walls and could be defended. The shortlived rebellion of Sacrovir in Gaul saw the capture of Augustodunum (Autun), chief town of the Aedui. But to find a parallel to the abandonment of Londinium in the face of the enemy, without any defence, one would have to go back to the rebellion of Vercingetorix, or to the wars against Mithridates. This and no other was the decision Suetonius now had to take. Tacitus tries to put it in the best possible light—'he decided to save the province as a whole by the sacrifice of a single city'. In fact, the price was to be two cities; the decision about Londinium settled the fate of Verulamium also. A limited evacuation was organized, as

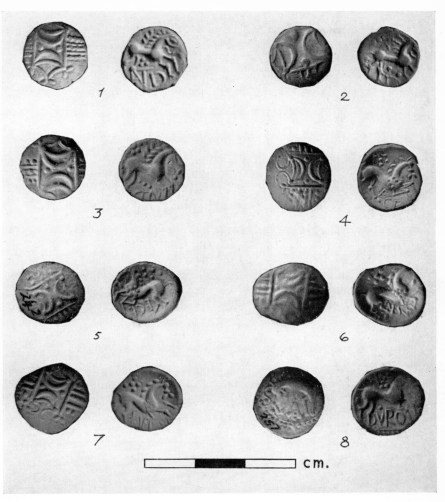

I. Some of the inscribed coins of the Iceni. 1. A͡NTD (420); 2. A͡NTD (422); 3. ICEN (424); 4. ECE (427); 5. ECE (420); 6. AESV (432); 7. SAEMV (433); 8. CA͡M DVRO (434). Numbers in brackets are Mack's classification.

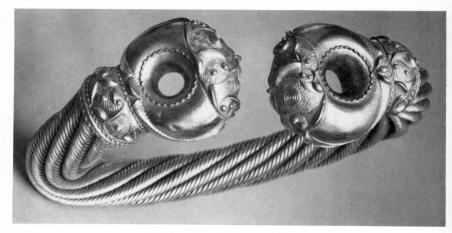

II. The Snettisham gold torc.

III. The model of a British war chariot based on fragments found in the Llyn Cerrig Bach hoard, Anglesey.

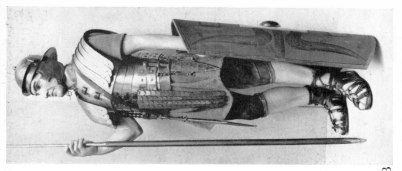

A

B

IV. A. Scene from Trajan's Column showing the Emperor being offered heads of the enemy by Gallic or British troops.
B. Full-size model of a Roman Legionary at the time of Trajan (in the Grosvenor Museum, Chester).

V. Tombstone of Facilis, a centurion of the
XXth Legion at Colchester.

VI. Tombstone of Longinus, a duplicarius of the first Thracian ala at Colchester.

VII. A model of the Temple of Claudius at Colchester.

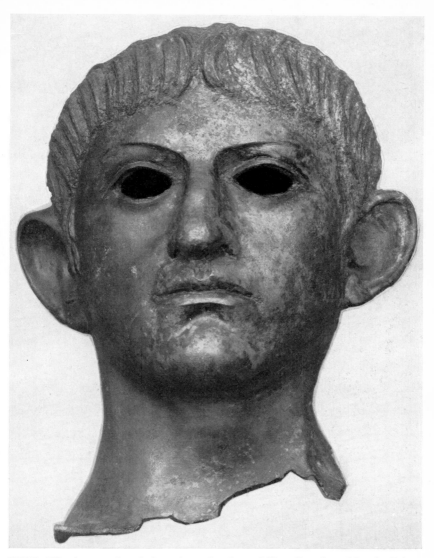

VIII. The bronze head thought to be that of Claudius found in the River Alde, Suffolk.

IX. A full-sized reconstruction of a corner tower of the fort at Metchley (Birmingham).

X. Excavations at Verulamium showing, marked by arrows, the thick layer of burnt debris of the destruction of the town during the revolt.

XI. The reconstructed tombstone of Classicianus in the British Museum.

XII. A crop mark showing a Roman fort near Wroxeter.

XIII. An aerial view of Watling Street looking west towards Wellington.

is clear from the phrase '*comitantes in partem agminis acciperet*' ('he took into his columns those ready to go with him').[1] But these would have been limited to men fit for active service, and, presumably, able to mount themselves; all Suetonius's strategy at this point depended on his being able to operate as a cavalry column. Women, children, and the old, together with those who could not leave the attractions of London (a little faded, one would have thought, at that juncture!) were left to their fate. There may have been some thought of ransoming them later; if so, it underrated the ferocity of Boudicca's men. So Suetonius withdrew his column north-westward from London, to fall back on his main forces advancing from Wales. It seems likely that he missed Boudicca's army by a narrow margin. Yet on that margin was to turn the whole issue of the war.

We now need to know how the situation looked to Boudicca. All Tacitus tells us about the Britons at this stage is that 'rejoicing in their spoil, and too lazy to undertake hardships, they left the forts and garrisons alone, and made for the places which offered the richest booty and were insecurely defended'. It is easy to understand that to keep control of a large native army, made up of many tribal contingents, and now drunk with success, was Boudicca's greatest problem. But an extremely able brain—hers or another's—had planned the opening phase of the campaign. What was its objective now? Suetonius must have surprised Boudicca by his unsupported cavalry dash to London. It looked, and was, hazardous in the extreme. But when the Britons had failed to cut him off, she must have been happy enough to see him in London, in the hope that the city would serve as a trap in which the Roman general would be caught and destroyed. Something other than the difficulty of concentrating her forces may account for Boudicca's delay in closing in on London. But then Suetonius made a second surprise move by withdrawing without any attempt at defence. Boudicca may have seen that the richest prize was the general, and he was beyond her reach for the moment; to her army, it was obviously London, and they moved in to take it. The massacre that followed, with its accompanying horrors, is described succinctly by Tacitus as 'slaughter, the gibbet, fire, and the cross'. Dio has a more detailed account of the atrocities perpetrated on women in the groves of Andrasta: 'their breasts were cut off and stuffed in their mouths, so that they seemed to be eating them, then their bodies were skewered lengthwise on sharp stakes'. Apologists of the British cause are prone to attempt to modify these atrocity stories, on the grounds that the name of Andrasta is unknown elsewhere in Celtic Britain, though paralleled by Andarta, a goddess of the Voconces in south-eastern Gaul. The offering of the heads of captives to the goddess of victory as her due after a battle would accord well with what is known of Celtic rites in Europe, and indeed as late as the ninth century we find references to the terrible triad of Irish goddesses of war and fertility, the Morrigan and her two companions.[2] But the Mau Mau bestiality of Dio's description may be a further clue to their purpose, taken in conjunction with a phrase of Tacitus that 'as though they were come to pay the penalty, they exacted vengeance in advance' (*'tamquam reddituri supplicium at praerepta interim ultione festinabant'*). Tacitus here has been unfairly attacked for forced rhetoric. In fact, the phrase is remarkable for its insight into psychology. The purpose of such actions—like the Mau Mau oath—is to compromise everyone, to leave no course open but a fight to the finish. We have seen too much of extremists in action in our times to fail to understand. So London went down in shame and agony.

Verulamium followed, perhaps within a few days. We need not assume, with Collingwood, that Suetonius took part in the same harrowing scene there as at London: although the quickest way to the north-west lay through it, he may have made the detour through Silchester, then north by Dorchester to Towcester. But when the Britons reached it there was the same disaster (*eadem clades municipio Verulamio fuit*), and the same horrors. We must pause to ask why. London was a city of merchants and business men—the *negotiatores* on whom the anger of oppressed provincials always fell heavily, as in the massacre of Roman *negotiatores* at Cenabum which triggered off the rising of Vercingetorix. But Verulamium was a cantonal capital, the chief city of the Catuvellauni, many of whom were in Boudicca's ranks. But it was a Romanized city; it had been accorded the title of *municipium*, the first city in Britain, in all probability, to be thus distinguished. The ferocity shown to its inhabitants by their fellow countrymen is a mark of the gulf that had opened up between the pro- and anti-Roman factions in the British states. The rebellion had now reached its highest point of success. The three chief cities of the province had been wiped out; their inhabitants, Roman and pro-Roman Britons, massacred to the number of some 70,000. It seems an astonishingly high figure, suggesting for London a population (inhabitants and refugees) of some 25,000–30,000. But Tacitus gives it as fact, using the word *'constitit'*—'it is established'. This certainly suggests the result of an inquiry, whether undertaken by Suetonius after the rebellion had collapsed, or by the commission sent out by Nero, one cannot say. It is, of course, true that such figures tend to be exaggerated, but perhaps, if we understand this one to include, not merely the three cities, but also pro-Romans in isolated farms, it is not wildly so.

These events were concentrated in a few summer weeks, perhaps no more than three. The next phase is more obscure, in place and time. Both Tacitus and Dio hurry on to the decisive battle, in which Suetonius broke the army of Boudicca in the field. Nothing but a few hints in their narrative makes it possible to divine something of the troop movements that took place and the strategy that lay behind them. For both sides, it would seem that food-supplies were crucial. Dio says that a shortage of food compelled Suetonius to give battle, against his judgement; Tacitus describes the Britons (after the great battle) as afflicted with famine, since they had deliberately omitted to sow their crops in the spring in the expectation of seizing Roman supplies. As often, Tacitus's explanation needs to be rounded out. To omit the spring sowing would mean that the hosting could take place several weeks earlier, and the rising get under way at a time when the Romans would not expect it. But it would have another purpose. Deprived of their supplies, and unable to live off the country, the Romans could not concentrate their forces in full strength, and would be brought to battle at a disadvantage. Two things went wrong with the British plan. The failure, already noted, to capture any Roman military positions made it possible for Suetonius to get some supplies and reinforcements. Later, after Boudicca's defeat and the break-up of her great army, the absence of supplies began to recoil on the Britons themselves, making it very difficult to keep up even a piecemeal existence.

Suetonius's problem must have been to concentrate the largest force he could maintain, and bring it to battle under conditions that would offset the huge British superiority in numbers. He would have two anxieties in sending for reinforcements: the first, to ensure that they were not overwhelmed by the enemy before they could join him; the second, to avoid weakening any vital position to an extent that would release a flood of new British adherents to Boudicca's cause. Tacitus's account of the Roman force that took part in the final battle makes it possible to see how this was done. 'He collected the XIVth Legion and detachments of the XXth, together with the nearest available auxiliaries, a total force of about 10,000 men.' The XIVth and XXth had been with the striking force in North Wales, the nearest available auxiliaries would be those from the forts in the Trent-Severn gap. The IXth at Lindum had already suffered a severe loss at the hands of Boudicca and was probably in no condition to take the field again, but it would play some role as a token force facing the Brigantes. For the same reason, it would seem likely that part of the XXth was left to guard against a threat from Wales or the north. The northern front held, and the main force of the Brigantes did not join the rebels. The difficulty is to understand the part played by the IInd Legion. It was absent from the final battle, and there would seem to be sound reason for leaving it at Glevum to mask the Silures, or indeed to hold a possible landing-place for reinforcements from the Continent. But it seems that communications had broken down with the commander-in-chief; if so, the failure of Postumus to keep the rendezvous with him on the march to London would mean that Suetonius regarded the whole legion as disloyal and left it out of his plans. Another possibility is that the legion had not yet been moved to Gloucester. There is some evidence from one of the south-western forts, Waddon Hill, near Beaminster in Dorset, that the military occupation continued into this period. If the legion was still in this area and some of its members divided up into splinter garrisons, as the evidence from Hod Hill clearly indicates, it puts a rather different complexion on the problem. Where was Suetonius during these weeks of planning and preparation? Here surely there can be little room for argument. Falling back from Verulamium on his advancing infantry, he would rejoin them somewhere about Venonae (High Cross) or Letocetum (Wall) and in this district was the ideal base for operations in the next phase. It was part of the defensive system in the Trent-Severn gap. Good communications led in four directions from this area, so that he could have drawn in supplies from the forces of the frontier zone. Equidistant from the Brigantian and Silurian frontiers, it offered the best hope there was of containing a break-through on either. Finally, and more important still, a base here would mean that Boudicca would have to come and find him, and at a place which he would choose. (Pl. XIII.)

It is less easy to see the situation from the British side. Boudicca had the problems common to all leaders of a Celtic confederate army. Hard to keep together in defeat, such a force was almost equally intractable after victory. It must have been no small achievement to round them up, call off the looting and burning, and move this great force north-west in search of Suetonius. Nine years earlier, Caratacus had staked all on a decisive battle—and lost. Boudicca had equally strong reasons for seeking a clash, and better prospects of success. For the Roman cause in Britain was now embodied in Suetonius and his army. Once he was eliminated, the demoralized IXth and IInd would soon be dealt with in turn, and the forts picked off in detail. And it was now or never. The Britons could not supply their huge army much longer, while to leave Suetonius at large into the winter would mean that he could get reinforcements through from the Continent before another campaigning season. Reason, one can hardly doubt, will have been reinforced by emotion. The ease with which they had brushed aside opposition at Colchester, the defeat of Cerialis, and the refusal of Suetonius to defend London and St. Albans, must have filled them with confidence in themselves and contempt for the Romans. Even before this, a British view of history seems to have regarded the Romans as by no means invincible. Above all, the withdrawal of Caesar had left a deep impression. Tacitus shows it as inspiring alike Caratacus in 51 and Calgacus

71

in 84. With this great example before them, and conscious, too, of the hesitations about staying in Britain which Nero's Government had recently entertained, Boudicca and her advisers might well have felt that the defeat of Suetonius would be the end of Roman power in Britain. 'Let us show them', Dio makes her say, 'that they are hares and foxes trying to rule over dogs and wolves.' Without taking Dio's rhetoric at its face value, we can well suppose that some such beliefs in their own superiority now buoyed up Boudicca and her men. So their huge army, grouped in its tribal contingents and with the wives of the warriors riding on waggons, went rolling through the Chilterns and on into the Midland forests.

In both Tacitus and Dio the account of the final battle is the dramatic climax of the Boudicca episode. Indeed, the conventions of classical historiography demand that this should be so. And for Tacitus, in particular, the decisive battle is a set-piece to call forth all his powers. Besides his British battle-pieces, Mons Graupius in the *Agricola*, the defeat of Caratacus, the victories of Suetonius over the Druids and over Boudicca, we must set compositions on an ampler scale—the battle of Idistaviso, or Bedriacum, Cremona, and the other battles of the year 69. Such events, in Tacitus's view, interest and stimulate the reader, and he wished that his chosen period had more of them to offer. Tacitus's battles follow a definite pattern. The rival armies are described, with their numbers, disposition, and arms. The speeches of the generals serve to reveal the motives with which each enters the contest—and to engage the interest of a public with a connoisseur's appreciation of rhetoric. Then follows the battle, the victory, and the casualties on either side, with sometimes a brief reference to some notable deed of valour. When the battle is with a foreign foe, Tacitus sheds all pretence of impartiality. The Roman commander is heir to Scipio and Caesar—he is often simply called *Romanus*—and the battle one of a glorious series going back to the early days of the Republic, and in most of which Rome had been victorious. Indeed, it would often be better if we could bring ourselves to accept Tacitus's battles on their own terms and to enjoy them as literary set-pieces; there is much they do not tell us that the modern military historian would like to know. The battle between Suetonius and Boudicca is a good example; we are left to guess when and where it took place. The time, it would seem, must have been the later summer or early autumn, and the place, somewhere between Towcester and Wall. Of one thing we can be sure, that Tacitus will have had a first-hand account of the battle from Agricola, who was then serving on Suetonius's staff and took part in it. This account he would condense, or dramatize, as he chose. But the basic facts must be there.

It must be supposed, from Tacitus's statement, that the battle took place on grounds of Suetonius's choosing, and that he

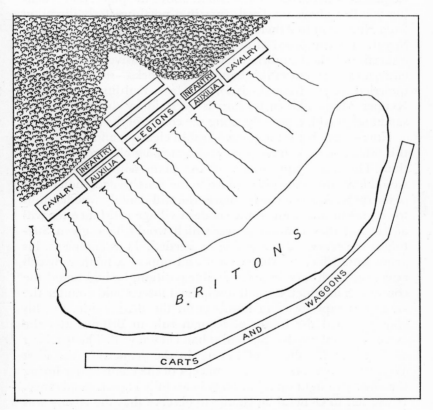

Fig. 4. The Battle between Suetonius and Boudicca.

would not move far from his base to find it. In other words, the neighbourhood of High Cross rather than Towcester is the place to look.[3] A narrow defile, protected by woods from the rear, and with a level plain in front offering no opportunity for ambushes, would not, one might suppose, preserve its features in the deforested and cultivated landscape of the modern Midlands. But one promising site may be put forward as at least meeting the conditions of the account of Tacitus. It is a suggestion, no more: it would be difficult to establish by excavation that it was, in fact, the site of the battle. In such cases, caution must be the first rule. But, with due caution, we draw attention to the escarpment which, rising some 200 ft. above the plain, and reaching 700 feet above sea-level, runs in a north-westerly direction from Nuneaton to Atherstone, where it converges with Watling Street. It is composed of the Stockingford shales and Hartshill quartzite of the Cambrian levels, with intrusive diorites. The eastern escarpment of this band of hard rocks—still extensively quarried for road-metal—is formed by a faultline against the Keuper Marl. This in its turn is overlaid by drift deposits of sand and gravel, especially along the course of the River Anker.

Now—and this is the point—before clearing and cultivation this fault line must have presented a striking change of vegetation. The heath appearance of the plain with its low scrub would have suddenly given place to the denser vegetation of the older rocks. Anyone who explores the still densely wooded hills to the north and west of the modern village of Mancetter will agree that they contain defiles which would have given Suetonius the rearward protection he needed. Thus anchored, his army would face Watling Street and oppose a further British advance. In this, or in some similar position, he had found the conditions in which a small disciplined force could counter the enormous superiority in numbers on the British side. On his choice turned the future of Roman rule in Britain, and the event was to show that Suetonius had chosen well. The teaching of all the staff colleges of Europe in the years after the First World War was based on the concept of the commander luring the enemy to fight on a battlefield carefully chosen in advance. It was left to General de Gaulle to observe that the enemy was not a fool and would be making a choice of his own. A fatal overconfidence led Boudicca to accept a pitched battle on her enemy's terms. To read Tacitus's account of the battles is to see how unjust is the charge that he is the most unmilitary of historians. He does not enable us to place the battle on the map, but—more important—he does give a clear picture of its course and character. The Romans occupied the defile, in dense formation, with the auxiliaries on their flanks, and cavalry massed on the wings. The immense British army—the largest which had ever been gathered—divided into its tribal contingents, and covered the open plain in front. At the rear was a kind of waggon-park, arranged to give the wives of the warriors a grandstand view of the slaughter. (So, eighteen centuries later, the ladies drove out in their carriages from Washington to watch the battle of Bull Run.) The noise of a great Celtic host, added to their known ferocity and their savage deeds at Londinium and Verulamium, must have been formidable to the waiting Romans. But Suetonius knew that superior equipment and discipline, given the chance to show themselves, would be decisive. 'Throw your javelins,' he told his men; 'strike with your short-swords and shield-bosses, carry on from there and mow them down. Don't think of booty: win the battle and you'll have everything.' It is advice that contains the basic formula for a small force confronting a larger but worse-equipped opponent. Extraordinary successes have been won in such circumstances—by Marius against the Cimbri, by Clive in India. Timing would be all important, and that of Suetonius was masterly. A Celtic charge was always formidable, but here it had to be made up a slope on to the Roman position. He waited until the very last minute before giving the order for the discharge of javelins,* which were then launched in two massive volleys with deadly effect. It was at this critical moment, when the British ranks were breathless and faltering, that the legionaries drew their swords and advanced swiftly in wedge-formation into the mass of Britons; the very weight of impact carrying them forward deep into their ranks and splitting them up. Here as on many another battlefield, the Roman stabbing-sword at close quarters had a deadly margin over the clumsy slashing sword of the Celts, who were further handicapped by

* 'Don't fire until you can see the whites of their eyes!'

their poor defensive armour. The legionary attack would have broken their army to pieces and spread them out, and they now were assaulted by the auxiliaries pressing in from the flanks. At a third stage, cavalry charges were launched on bands of Britons trying to extricate themselves from the mêlée. At this point, according to Tacitus, the British force broke and turned to flight. Dio tells a different story: a day-long struggle of swaying fortunes, with the British chariots getting in some effective rushes until they were dispersed by concentrated fire from the Roman archers. Tacitus tends to telescope his battles and it may be that here Dio is to be preferred, for even to butcher so large an army would have been a long job for Suetonius's men. But the last phase of the engagement is clear. Their own waggons proved a fatal obstacle to the defeated Britons. Killing the draught-oxen and overturning the waggons, the Romans trapped part of the British force in front of them and cut them down to a man—indeed, to judge from Tacitus, to a woman as well. It was this that led to the enormous disparity in casualties—80,000 killed on the British side, 400 on the Roman, with many more wounded. Neither figure, perhaps, is to be taken very seriously, but we cannot dissent from Tacitus's verdict—'It was a famous victory, equal to those of ancient times.' It was indeed—equal to that of Marius at Aquae Sextiae, or some of Caesar's victories in Gaul.

Suetonius had done all he could have hoped for—except to capture Boudicca. She escaped from the battle, and it seems that she got back to her own kingdom. But the confederacy was shattered, and the Romans would be sure to hunt her down. Her own conduct of the war had made it impossible to hope for the *clementia* that had been shown to Caratacus. Life had nothing more for her, and she ended it by taking poison.* Like Cleopatra, the British warrior queen had no mind to figure in a Roman triumph. To her death Dio adds an interesting postscript, that 'the Britons mourned her deeply and gave her a costly burial'. It is tempting to ask where this information came from. As the last ruler of her house, it is likely that the Royal treasure (what was left of it!) would be buried with her. No doubt this would be done secretly, but the Romans would

* Tacitus, xiv, 37. Dio says she died of a disease.

certainly look for her grave, for they would not allow any memorial of Boudicca to survive. Did they find it when, a few months later, the territory of the Iceni was ravaged with fire and sword?

For Poenius Postumus, the news of the battle also came to clarify his problems. He had failed his commander, broken his oath, and made a bad situation infinitely worse. And now his own soldiers—whatever they may have said or felt earlier—were loud in their complaints that they had been cheated of the glory won by the XIVth and XXth. But Romans of the first century at least knew how to die. Poenius Postumus fell on his sword.

Suetonius's victory had been decisive in one sense, that it had broken the great British confederacy and re-established the Roman hold on the province. Rebellion now was on a tribal basis, but there was much to be done before it could be put down. The machinery of Roman government must be set going again, the army brought up to strength after the losses it had sustained, tribes still in arms brought to heel and punished according to their deserts. Beyond these immediate problems lay the larger question of the whole nature of Roman policy in Britain. For a disaster equal to the Boudicca rebellion in any province of the Empire, one would have to go back half a century to the great rising in Pannonia and Dalmatia under Augustus. Neither the revolt of Tacfarinas in Africa, nor that of Florus and Sacrovir in Gaul, the two chief risings of Tiberius' reign, were on anything like the same scale. The Britons were far less tractable than had been supposed; if Roman rule was to be successful in the future, it would be necessary to find governors with something more than the military virtues. Suetonius and his friends might bask in the glory of having recovered the province (*recuperatae provinciae gloria*): to the Imperial Government it might seem more significant that he had so nearly lost it.

Meanwhile there could be no thought of superseding him in the first flush of victory. Reinforcements were sent out from the Rhine army, the great reserve against emergencies in the western provinces. Two thousand legionaries brought the IXth up to strength again; there were also eight cohorts of auxiliaries—probably the eight Batavian cohorts whom Tacitus mentions elsewhere (*Hist.*, IV, 12), as having served in Britain under their own chieftains. There was further a cavalry *ala* of 1,000 men, a highly mobile and rare type of unit. With these reinforcements Suetonius was ready to crush the last embers of defiance, and the rebellion moved into its final protracted agony. 'The whole army was concentrated, and kept in tents to finish the war.' Tacitus's phrase means, presumably, that only token forces were left in the west and north, and every man that could be spared moved to the areas affected by the rebellion. 'Now winter quarters were found for the auxiliary cohorts and cavalry, and the territory of every single state that had been disloyal or unreliable was laid waste with fire and sword.' No certain traces of this great deployment of force can be confirmed by archaeological evidence, although it must have extended over the whole of eastern England from Colchester to Lincoln, and devastated rebellious territory with a thoroughness equal to the Harrying of the North by William the Conqueror. And yet British resistance was still being maintained, and indeed lasted at least until the spring of 61. Its main strength now derived from the fear inspired by the personality of Suetonius himself, from his harshness towards all who surrendered and his determination to exact revenge for every single wrong—and there had been plenty. It is not hard to find parallels for such a situation in our own time. For a solution, new men and a fresh point of view would have to be found.

C. Julius Alpinus Classicianus was the man chosen by the Imperial Government to succeed Catus Decianus as *procurator* and to take a new, hard look at the British problem. He must have reached the province in the autumn of 60, at the same time as the military reinforcements, and, like them, he came from the Rhineland. His wife was the daughter of Julius Indus, a pro-Roman noble of the state of the Treveri, who had played a great part in crushing the rebellion roused by Julius Florus amongst that people in A.D. 21, and, later, in securing a just peace. To his daughter, born, presumably, at about this time, he gave the name of Pacata, 'the child of peace'. Classicianus himself was a member of a prominent family of the Treveri, the Alpinii; Birley has shown that his membership of the Fabian tribe, attested by his epitaph, means that he must have acquired

Roman citizenship in the reign of Tiberius or Gaius, i.e. not later than 41, and probably earlier than 37. He would be, then, a man in his forties, or perhaps older, when he came to Britain. He could see both the Roman and the provincial point of view, and believed that they could be reconciled to produce justice and civilization. It was a good choice for this difficult situation. For, though Classicianus would be responsible for re-establishing the day-to-day financial administration of the province, there can be little doubt that he was really sent to investigate the reasons for the rebellion and report. As *procurator*, he would be in direct communication with the Emperor, and free to conduct whatever enquiry he chose.

It is easy to believe that governor and *procurator* soon found themselves at odds. For several months Suetonius had had to act in Britain on his own responsibility, without help from the Central Government. He and his men had retrieved a desperate situation through their own exertions, and it would be natural if they had developed a very strong *esprit de corps* in so doing. Indeed, its traces are clearly to be seen in the Tacitean account of the rebellion, even though it was written more than forty years later. And part of the reward that Suetonius promised his army—and that they had promised themselves—was a thorough and adequate vengeance for all the British atrocities. He would have little time for talk of moderation, coming from a man who had never seen the skewered Roman women at Londinium. As for Classicianus, he was appalled by what he found. Revenge, rather than reconstruction, was the keynote of the governor's policy; unconditional surrender all that he had to offer. In such cases excess leads to excess, and nothing seemed to lie ahead but the barren prospect of endless destruction. The famous reproach of Calgacus to the Romans 'they make a desert, and call it peace', would serve well to describe what Suetonius was doing at this time. Tacitus, in recounting the breach between the two chief Roman officials in Britain, does not hesitate to impute disloyalty to Classicianus, who 'allowed his private quarrels to stand in the way of the public interest, since he let it be known that it would be wise to wait for a new governor, who, lacking the anger of an enemy or the arrogance of a conqueror, would be disposed to show mercy to those who gave themselves up'. The public interest, we may confidently suppose, would be much better served by Classicianus's advice, repeated several times during the autumn and winter of 60/61, that no end of hostilities could be foreseen unless Suetonius was replaced.

These reports must have caused acute embarrassment to Nero's administration. We have already noted the enthusiasm evoked by the Neronian forward policy in both east and west, and how eagerly the Roman public followed the doings of Corbulo and Suetonius, the rival generals. Corbulo on the eastern front had undoubtedly a more consistent record. The troops he took over in Syria—unlike the battle-hardened legions of Britain—had become demoralized with the easy conditions of service in that province. There were among them veterans who had never stood guard nor wielded a pick: 'smooth moneymakers' is Tacitus's contemptuous phrase. Corbulo had on his hands a job of toughening up that would have gladdened the heart of a Montgomery. These unmilitary characters were routed out of the taverns and brothels of Syria, the most hopeless of them discharged, and new levies brought in from the highland districts of Asia, as well as units from the German frontier. Then the whole force was transported to the bleak plateau of Erzerum, to pass a winter under canvas at 6,000 feet above sea-level. What survived was an army, and with it Corbulo, in the years 58 and 59, and in some of the roughest country in Asia, achieved results unsurpassed by any Roman commander of the early Empire, and culminating in the capture of Artaxata and Tigranocerta, the two capitals of Armenia. Corbulo's brilliant successes in 59 had been matched, to a degree at least, by what Suetonius has achieved in Wales; but then the disasters of the Boudicca rebellion had followed, a severe setback to Suetonius' prestige and to that of the Government itself. Now it had all been retrieved by a resounding victory like those of former times. To recall a governor with his task still unfinished—but thus far so nobly advanced—would be out of the question. Further investigation was called for, and further advice as to what might be possible. To provide it, a full-scale Commission of Inquiry was sent to Britain, headed by the freedman, Polyclitus.

The custom of employing freedmen in important public affairs began with Augustus, but only developed on a large scale under Claudius. In his reign came the organization of an Imperial Civil Service with five major departments, each under the control of a freedman. Like so many features of the Early Empire, it was really an extension of a practice which had long prevailed in great Roman households, where freedmen of Greek or Oriental origin were often given important responsibilities in the management of the estate. Under Claudius freedmen attained an unprecedented degree of influence, and much of the secret history of his Court turned on the rivalries and intrigues of Pallas and Narcissus. Needless to say, the Roman aristocracy hated such men, and the senatorial tradition, represented in Tacitus, always portrays them as arrogant, avaricious, and corrupt. In his earlier years Nero had made a promise to limit the employment of freedmen to his private affairs, and not to use them in affairs of state. But the promise was not kept. In his reign, four successive Prefects of Egypt were men of this order, and others are found in such important posts as Prefect of the Praetorian Guard and Prefect of the Corn Supply (*praefectus annonae*)—both offices of the first rank. During his absence in Greece (66–68) Nero left Italy in charge of the freedman Helius. His administration is mentioned by several writers as notoriously venal and avaricious, and Polyclitus was one of his associates at this time. The influence—and perhaps the lives—of all these men cannot have survived Nero's murder in 68. It is easy to see why the Emperor should find freedmen so useful. Intelligent, adaptable, free from the prejudices and rivalries of the aristocracy, owing an exclusive loyalty to him, they were invaluable for confidential affairs. Nor is it hard to see how Suetonius must have felt about the mission of Polyclitus. Classicianus was bad enough, but this was worse. Men holding responsible posts do not, in our own times, normally welcome a Royal Commission appointed to inquire into their activities—but at least the members of such a Commission are not usually social inferiors and aliens. The prejudice with which Tacitus writes about Polyclitus is so obvious that it is surprising to find modern commentators so often deceived by it. We are told of the burden caused to Italy and Gaul through billeting his huge train of attendants: he travelled, it would seem, on a lavish expense account. In a senator, of course, a long train of attendants would have been a mark of *dignitas* and *auctoritas*, for which the provincials ought to have been honoured to pay. His mission was not merely to heal the breach between the governor and procurator, but also to win over the still intransigent Britons to a peace settlement. The unsophisticated Britons laughed at him, says Tacitus, not realizing what the power of a freedman was. (Did they stir a flicker of sympathy in Suetonius?) But, in fact, Polyclitus's mission seems to have been successful. The report he sent in was very much toned down, according to Tacitus, who would no doubt have liked to see an open condemnation of Classicianus. We can do little more than speculate as to how it was received and considered in Rome. Nero was in the twenty-third year of his life, and the sixth of his reign. It was already stained by two great dynastic crimes—the murder of his stepbrother Britannicus in 55, and that of his mother Agrippina in 59. But although the famous five years of good government (54–59) were over, the ministers responsible for it, Seneca and Burrus, were still in power. The death of Burrus in 62 is usually regarded as the turning-point in Nero's reign, and the Terror which marked its last phase is ascribed, above all, to the influence of his successor as Prefect of the Praetorian guard, Tigellinus. In 60 Nero had already made the fatal discovery that there was no limit to his power, and in any political objective on which he set his heart—such as his mother's death—he had his way. But artistic ambitions and private vices still interested him more than public affairs. It is unlikely that he took much time off from these for Classicianus's report—nor was there as yet a regularly constituted *Consilium Principis* or Privy Council, as later under Hadrian. A number of influential men, known as *amici Caesaris*, were consulted from time to time, but not as members of a formal body. Executive power was still in the hands of Seneca and Burrus, and it is virtually certain that the decision would be taken by them. Both men came from provincial families of equestrian status; Seneca, from one of the great wealth in Spain, Burrus from a poor family in Gallia Narbonensis. Their administration had shown care for the provinces, and anxiety to restrain the abuses of governors. Only recently (59) had they tried to formulate a far-reaching scheme for the reform of taxation, which had been much pared down after discussion in the Senate. We do not know precisely how far these factors of background and outlook affected them on their judgement of Suetonius. And their decision would, of course, be confidential. But we can fairly deduce its main recommendations from the steps taken by the Government. Suetonius was, for the time being, to be kept in charge of Britain, probably on the grounds that the army would be outraged by his immediate recall. None the less, a change of policy in Britain was imperative: he must go at the first convenient opportunity; and a successor be sent out to pursue a conciliatory line.

It so happened that in this winter of 60/61 Nero's Government had also to make a major change of policy on the eastern front. Corbulo's successes in Armenia had made it possible to place a Roman nominee, Tigranes, on the throne of that kingdom, but he was unable to look after himself, and some other solution had to be found. The decision seems to have been taken to turn Armenia into a Roman province; leaving Corbulo in his Syrian command to watch the Parthians, a new general was required for Cappadocia as a springboard for an Armenian campaign. Before the end of the winter policy had been decided, and the consuls of the year 61 had been chosen to carry it out. Forward in Armenia, under Caesennius Paetus, standstill in Britain under Petronius Turpilianus. They would hold the consulship for a few months only—four, at the most—and would be available for employment in the late spring. At about that time Suetonius suffered a convenient setback—the loss, according to Tacitus, of a few ships and their complement on the coast. We do not know where this was, but it is tempting to connect it with operations against the Iceni, for a recent excavation at Thornham suggests that their last stand was made on the north Norfolk coast. Tacitus plays down the incident, and it may have been more serious than he suggests. At all events, it was used by the Government as a pretext to recall Suetonius, and Petronius Turpilianus was sent out to replace him. A new chapter in the history of Roman Britain had begun.

5

AFTERMATH

SOMETIMES WE CAN POINT OUT the injustices of history to individuals, but lack the means to set things right. The last two
Neronian governors of Britain, Petronius Turpilianus and M.
Trebellius Maximus, and to some extent their Vitellian successor, Vettius Bolanus, are in just such a case. Between them,
their governorship covered ten years, a period in which the
situation in Britain was transformed out of recognition. In 61
the province was still mutinous, ruined, and exhausted. Ten
years later, with Vespasian firmly in control after the termination of the Civil Wars of 69, it was loyal enough to serve as a
firm base for a new and far-reaching forward policy. In the
space of some fifteen years (71–85), and under three governors of
high ability, first northern England, and then the whole of
Wales, were subjugated and brought within Roman control.
The third and final phase was to have been the conquest of
Scotland—the grand objective of Agricola's ambitions. It was
never completed—neither by him nor anyone else. But at least
he explored the country and its coastline, penetrated its mountain recesses, won a pitched battle against its united forces, and
showed that its conquest was perfectly feasible—if it was thought
to be worth while.

It is beyond the scope of this book to tell the details of these
years of military advance. They were accompanied by something even more important, a coherent and successful policy
of Romanization in the civil areas of the province which
yielded lasting results. Brigantia, it is true, gave trouble from
time to time, but there were no more nationalist uprisings

in the old Claudian province—no successor to Boudicca.

It calls for no great historical insight to deduce that the foundations of both the military conquest and of the Romanization of the province were laid in the quiet, unspectacular work of the Roman administration during the ten years which may properly be called the aftermath of the great rebellion. But to support this deduction by chapter and verse is something we cannot yet do: perhaps it will never be possible, unless the exploration of Romano-British town sites gives substantial new evidence of development that belongs to these years. The historical evidence—need it be said?—is dominated by the picture of Tacitus, who has obtained the effects he wanted in two ways. The work of the Neronian governors is passed over, and the men themselves belittled. Again, all credit for the policy of Romanization goes to the Flavian governors, and, especially, to Agricola. Let us consider what he says, and then see how far we can get behind it. First, the men. Twice[1] Petronius Turpilianus is dismissed in a single sentence. In the first we are told that 'himself unprovoked, and without provoking the enemy, he gave the honourable name of peace to a period of sluggish inaction'. In the second, 'new to the enemy's crimes, and therefore more kindly disposed towards repentence, he settled the former disorders, attempted nothing further, and handed over the province to Trebellius Maximus': *compositis prioribus*—if in his governorship of three years Petronius Turpilianus had really settled the aftermath of the rebellion, the ablative absolute may be called one of the most absolute in Latin! That the Roman Government thought his work satisfactory is shown by the fact that he was awarded the *insignia triumphalia*[2] on his return, in pointed contrast to the treatment of Suetonius Paulinus. Of his later career we know only that he held the important office of *curator aquarum*, President of the Water Board, and that, as a faithful supporter of Nero, he was murdered by Galba in 68.[3] Trebellius Maximus[4] was, to an even greater degree, one of those hopelessly unmilitary characters whom Tacitus found so uncongenial. He had been consul in 55 or 56, but his career had included no military experience. The appointment of such a man, one might think, was in itself a tribute to the thoroughness of Petronius Turpilianus's work.

Of his administration in Britain, which extended over six years
(63–69) we are told two things. Towards the Britons he practised 'a genial style of administration' (*comitate quadam curandi*),
which they appreciated, 'for the barbarians had by now learned
to be tolerant of attractive vices'. Well they might—such a
policy must have been a welcome novelty. But from the Roman
army in Britain, Trebellius could command neither loyalty nor
respect. 'Accustomed to campaigns, the troops got out of hand
in idleness.' This was common enough with Roman armies, and
it was probably aggravated by the presence of a number of
fire-eaters among the senior officers, a legacy of Suetonius
Paulinus. The usual cure was a strenuous programme of work
on frontier defences or canals, but we hear of nothing of the
kind. Moreover, Trebellius is said to have earned their contempt through 'greed and meanness'—*per avaritiam et sordes*.[5] It
is tempting to read into this an attempt to discourage the various
forms of racketeering and peculation open to the Roman army
in a province, and which both Agricola and Corbulo put down
with a firm hand. Twice Trebellius found himself faced with a
rebellion among his troops. The first—undated—was put down
without bloodshed by what Tacitus calls a disgraceful bargain
—'the general getting his life, the army liberty to do as it
liked'. The second was more serious. Roscius Coelius, the
commander of the XXth Legion, had been a ringleader against
the governor in the earlier mutiny. The Civil Wars gave him a
fresh opportunity, for now the army in Britain was isolated.
Roscius Coelius proceeded to gather military forces to further
his own ambitions—as was being done all over the Roman
world in that year of A.D. 69. He was joined by a number of
auxiliary units, cavalry and infantry, presumably those adjacent to the XXth Legion. No force came to the governor's
support, and he fled overseas to join the cause of Vitellius. He
had hoped to be replaced in his command, but—perhaps with
good reason—Vitellius disappointed him. The whole episode is
of interest as showing how a policy that favoured the interests
of the provincials could clash with those of the army. This we
must concede to Tacitus, that only a governor able to keep a
firm hand on the army could, at this period, really make a
success of Britain.

Vettius Bolanus,[6] if we follow his account, was not such a man. 'He did not harrass Britain by military efficiency . . .', but the soldiers liked him, and one military episode in his time—an intervention in Brigantian affairs to rescue Cartimandua—was handled efficiently. But in the case of Bolanus there is evidence other than that of Tacitus, and Professor Eric Birley[7] has shown how it may be used to put his governorship in a very different light, and to credit him with the first effective push into Caledonia. If so, he laid the foundations for the enduring work of Petilius Cerialis in the north.

The broad outlines of the policy followed by these three governors towards the provincials are reasonably clear. Details elude us. Financial problems must have been the most immediate. Abuses by the Roman financial officers had driven the Britons to rebellion: their distress must have been heightened by the months of warfare, and the destruction that followed. Fortunately, Classicianus was *procurator*. His task must have been formidable. The whole taxation system of the province would need to be investigated, abuses cut out, and a new spirit introduced into its working. Many of the Britons must have been ruined; there must have been much writing off of arrears. The burning of tax-commissioners' ledgers—so gratifying a feature of sculptured panels of one of the balustrades in the Forum Romanum[8]—may well have taken place in Britain. How long Classicianus had for his work of healing we do not know. He died in Britain; almost certainly, in office.[9] But at least we can be confident that his work was well done, and that its effects were lasting. When Tacitus describes the reforms of Agricola at the beginning of his governorship in A.D. 78, he does indeed mention a number of financial rackets that were brought to an end. But the significant thing is that these were all abuses practised by members of the governor's staff; nothing is said about the *procurator*.[10] Had there been any corruption on that side that called for Agricola's intervention, Tacitus would hardly have passed it over—he had no liking for procurators. It seems a safe inference, then, that the reforms introduced by Classicianus were still working well nearly twenty years later. If so, Collingwood was surely right in regarding him as 'the real hero of the story' of the Boudicca rebellion, and in claiming his tombstone, now in the British Museum, as 'a permanent possession of the British nation.'[11] (Pl. XI.)

The work of Classicianus made possible the other major aspect of the new policy in Britain—the drive for full-scale Romanization. What this implied is set out in a *locus classicus* in the *Agricola* of Tacitus.[12] There, of course, Tacitus claims the whole credit for Agricola, and dates the adoption of the policy narrowly to the second winter of his governorship, the winter of A.D. 79-80. Both claims may safely be rejected. Agricola's governorship may well have been an intensive phase of Romanization. But that process was far from complete even in the reign of Hadrian; equally, its beginning may reasonably be pushed back to the period A.D. 61-71. With these reservations, the passage deserves the most careful study. 'The following winter', says Tacitus, 'was devoted to beneficial policies. To ensure that men who, because they were uncivilized and lived in isolated dwellings, were easily roused to warfare, should grow used to peace and leisure, he would encourage them personally, and provide public grants, to build temples, *fora*, and town houses. The obedient met with praise, the sluggish with censure, and so a competition for honour served instead of compulsion. Indeed, he took in hand the provision of a liberal education for the sons of the nobles, expressing a preference for British abilities (when trained) to those of the Gauls. As a result, those who had once rejected the Latin language became anxious to excel at rhetoric. The next stage was that Roman dress became fashionable, the toga was often to be seen; little by little, there was a relapse into demoralizing luxuries, such as colonnades, hot baths, sumptuous dinner-parties. This, thought unsophisticated Britons, is civilization, really, it was a mark of their servitude.' Setting aside the irony so characteristic of Tacitus, here is an admirably succinct description of the process of Romanization, not merely in Britain, but in the western provinces as a whole. Its vehicle is the city, the chief civilizing agency of the Mediterranean world, its object, the native aristocracy. Bring them away from the deep countryside and its Celtic ways, put them in towns, give them a Roman education, expose them to urban amenities. There was nothing new about this policy. We can watch it at work on a larger canvas in Tres Galliae, where it was first set in motion by Julius Caesar, and greatly extended by Augustus. It is true that the brilliant and varied urban civilization of the old province of Narbonensis—'more Italy than province'— could not be developed in these northern and western lands. Instead there grew up a blend of Roman and Celtic institutions, whose basis was the old Celtic tribal unit—the *civitas*—itself irradiated by Romanizing influences deriving from its capital city, often a new foundation. Such were, for example, in Belgica, Durocortorum (Reims) for the Remi, Augusta Suessionum (Soissons) for the Suessiones; in Aquitania, Augustonemeton (Clermont-Ferrand) for the Arverni, and Vesunna (Périgueux) for the Petrucorii. From literature and from archaeology we can form an adequate idea of the cultural role of such centres as Augustodunum (Autun) among the Aedui, or Augusta Treverorum (Trèves) among the Treveri. Augustodunum,[13] founded in 12 B.C. to replace the old hill-fort of Bibracte (Mont Beuvray), became a rich and splendid city, famous especially for the school founded there for the education of the sons of the nobility of all Gaul. When Sacrovir captured the city in the rising of 21, these youths were held as hostages.[14] In the third century the school was still in existence, and funds were raised to restore it after its destruction by the Bagaudae. At Trèves[15] we see the sequence of a Celtic *oppidum*, a civilian settlement, developing from an auxiliary fort, and renamed Augusta Treverorum, and the Claudian colony of A.D. 44–45, whose street-pattern can still be traced. Already *urbs opulentissima* by the middle of the first century A.D., it superseded Reims as the greatest city of Gallia Belgica, and became one of the imperial capitals of the Late Empire. Gaul, too, will show us the role of education. Besides that at Autun, there were famous schools at Reims, Vienne, Bordeaux, Trèves, and Lyons. Caligula founded oratorical contests, in both Greek and Latin, and presumably for all three provinces, at Lyons.[16] The Gauls had a natural gift for rhetoric, known to the Romans as early as the second century B.C. In the Empire men of Gallic origin, such as Domitius Afer and Favorinus of Arles, were among the most famous orators of their times—though both, admittedly, came from Narbonensis. All but one of the orators in Tacitus' *Dialogus* came from Gaul. If, then, Agricola really thought the

Britons had it in them to do better than their neighbours, he was setting an extremely high standard. We know of nothing to suggest that they ever attained it.

What Tacitus has described was therefore no new policy, sprung fully-fledged from the brain of Agricola during the winter of A.D. 79–80, but rather a well-tried system with a long history in the western provinces. In the reign of Claudius, Corbulo had used it, on a small scale, among the Frisii on the Lower Rhine. Yet there is a sense in which it was new to Britain, and which seems to mark a decisive break with Claudian policy in the province. This is in the scale on which it was conceived and the systematic way in which it was applied. Claudius, after all, had been chiefly concerned with the Belgic kingdom, the *regnum* of Cunobelinus. The foundation of the colony at Camulodunum, the granting of municipal status to Verulamium, were measures intended to promote its Romanization, while the Temple of Claudius and its priesthood were to affect the nobility of the entire province. Claudius was given a free hand by the Senate in his dealings with the Britons after the conquest, and Mr. A. L. F. Rivet[17] has recently pointed out that we know very little of the arrangements made with such important *civitates* as, for example, the Dobunni or the Cornovii. We have seen that he granted loans, and he may have hoped that these would be used to further Romanization. By Cogidubnus at Noviomagus they certainly were, but other examples would be hard to quote. But the new policy adopted, if we are right, as a result of the lessons of the Boudicca rebellion, involved the official promotion of Romanization throughout the province. Thus the Brigantes are provided with a capital at Isurium (Aldborough) immediately after their conquest: the same with the Silures at Caerwent: shortly after A.D. 70 the Iceni were encouraged to make what seems to be a fresh start at Venta Icenorum (Caistor). In fact the only areas of Britain in which the cantonal system and some measure of urban development does not appear are those of three of the tribes of Wales, the Ordovices, the Degeangi, and Demetae. If Mr. Rivet's suggestion is right, and Moridunum (Carmarthen) was the administrative centre of the Demetae, perhaps in North Wales alone did urban life never develop at all. Small-scale

though urbanization of Roman Britain might be, compared
with that of Spain or Gaul, it was pursued with resolution. It
is true that there is, as yet, little archaeological evidence that
can be firmly dated to the decade 61-71. The bath-building at
Silchester appears to belong to this period: there was also
vigorous reconstruction of private property at Verulamium,
though the Forum belongs to the governorship of Agricola. A
number of villas, notably in Catuvellaunian territory, were
rebuilt or enlarged at this time. The educational side of the new
policy we can hardly document at all. Was there an official
foundation of a school for the sons of chieftains, a parallel to the
famous school of Autun? Something of the kind would be
needed to break the hold of the Druids on education. Or were
schools promoted in each of the cantonal capitals? If so, where
did the schoolmasters come from? Juvenal says that the Gauls
taught the Britons rhetoric: were the first Latin masters in
Britain—parents of a long and honourable posterity—also
fetched from across the Channel? Our evidence for what must
have been a major educational development amounts to a few
snippets, such as that, in the time of Agricola, a Greek rhetori-
cian called Demetrius of Tarsus found it worth his while to
make a British tour.[18]

As in education, so in language. We can describe the con-
testants, British and Latin, we know rather more about the
results, but we cannot recapture the details of the conflict.
Indeed, it is sobering to reflect that we should know so little
about this major issue of the life of Roman Britain, though
archaeology is able to recover so much of its material aspect,
even down to the trivial bric-à-brac of daily life. Fortunately,
there is a magisterial survey of the whole linguistic problem in
Professor K. H. Jackson's *Language and History in Early Britain*.[19]
He shows that while Latin was the language of administration,
both central and local, of justice, of the army, and of large-scale
commerce, and therefore a necessary part of education for the
upper classes, the British language and the native culture per-
sisted in the highland zone and among the peasantry. It is
easy to draw the wrong conclusion from the fact that there is
not a single inscription in British: Latin was the written language, and if the *graffiti* of Roman Britain are in Latin, it does

not follow that those who write them habitually spoke Latin. To an observer who looked ahead from the start of the conflict between Latin and British, the final victory of Latin might not seem in doubt. But, in Britain, the issue of the clash of languages was the opposite of that in Gaul. There, the Celtic language had everywhere disappeared before the end of the Roman period, leaving the more or less classical Latin of the schools, and the vulgar Latin of daily life, to become the progenitors of the Romance languages of France. In Britain the Celtic language, enriched, it is true, by some 800 Latin loan-words, outlived the Roman period, and its direct descendant, modern Welsh, is spoken today by more than seven hundred thousand people. With the possible exception of Basque, no other such survival is known in any of the lands which were once the western provinces of the Roman Empire. But the Celtic language never developed a written literature in Roman times in this island; it is from the early Dark Ages that we must date the beginning of that noble Welsh literature which has continued unbroken to the present day. Thus the language and literature of Wales came to form a major part of that splendid Celtic heritage, which, at the present time, is so grossly undervalued by the people of Britain.

So far, we have spoken of the aftermath of the rebellion in general terms. But, of course, events of this magnitude leave an indelible impression on the lives of the individuals who take part in them. And there are three persons, at least—all Romans —for whose later career there is enough evidence to be worth recounting. Least interesting is the case of Suetonius Paulinus. In the years immediately after his recall he must have been an awkward problem for Nero's administration. As 'the man who had finished off a great war' (*tanti belli confector*) his reputation was high in army circles and with the Roman people, yet he had been recalled in semi-disgrace. It would seem that he was skilfully handled. There was no bestowal of *insignia triumphalia* nor, it would seem, of any other official distinction; on the other hand, his political career was not brought to an end. After a decent interval—which he probably employed in the writing of his *Memoirs*[20]—he became consul for the second time in 66. In the Civil Wars of 69 he was a leading adherent of

Otho; as the oldest man of consular rank, and with a fine military reputation, his advice carried weight. He was chosen by Otho as one of the three generals to defend north Italy against the advance of Vitellius with the Rhine armies. Faced with Roman troops commanded by Roman generals, he did not repeat his successes in Mauretania and Britain. Tacitus[21] represents him as overcautious: 'he always preferred cautious policies founded on reason to flashy successes gained by chance.' So, at the battle of Locus Castrorum, his caution prevented his side from gaining a more decisive victory. Before the fatal battle of Bedriacum, we find him urging that Otho had everything to gain by postponing action. It is interesting to read that he employed among his arguments the desirability of waiting for the arrival of the XIVth Legion, the famous legion with which he had won his victory over Boudicca, and which in 66 had been transferred from Britain for service in Dalmatia. Suetonius Paulinus was an old man now, with an old man's liking for the familiar. Otho was twenty-seven, a gambler and a voluptuary, and inclined to put it to the touch to win or lose it all. He lost: and with the ruin of the Othonian cause Suetonius made his peace with Vitellius by rather dishonourable arguments and passes out of history.

Greater interest attaches to the later career of Petilius Cerialis. The events of 69 led him to support his fellow countryman Vespasian, and to display his talents on a larger stage. Still in his early forties, he had lost none of his energy or recklessness, nor indeed his gift for escaping from a tricky position—political, military, or amorous.[22] As soon as Vespasian had defeated Vitellius he was given a major command, and sent to deal with the very dangerous sitation that had been precipitated in Gaul and Germany by the Civilis rebellion. We cannot recount that highly complex story,[23] but no study of Boudicca can neglect some aspects of what may be called its pathology. The people of Gaul and Germany followed with keen attention the terrible struggles between the contending Roman factions. To some the collapse of Roman power seemed at hand. The legions on the Rhine were depleted: the governor of Upper Germany, Hordeonius Flaccus, old and incompetent. Among the tribes, old rivalries revived, new ambitions and messianic hopes began to gain ground. In the burning of the Capitol, the Druids of Gaul saw the sign of the end of Roman power, and of the transfer of the mastery of the world in the northern peoples.[24] A mysterious prophetess, Veleda, inspired the rebellion of Civilis;[25] she lived in a high tower in the depths of the Westphalian forest, and foretold the success of the German cause. Earlier, the small Celtic tribe of the Boii had produced a messiah of their own, Mariccus,[26] who headed a 'mob of fanatics', eight thousand strong; he was captured and thrown to the wild beasts in the arena at Vienne, but they would not touch him. As in the Boudicca rebellion, the role of the native religions in fomenting anti-Roman feelings is to be noted. Against this apocalyptic background the rebellious leaders pursued their own political ends. Those of Civilis, the Batavian leader, were simple enough. He wanted to free his people from their dependence on the Romans, especially their obligation to military service, and to build up for himself a powerful empire. Among the Gallic tribes of the Treveri and the Lingones something more complex took shape. They were led into rebellion by men of the old Royal house,[27] but who were themselves deeply Romanized from serving among the auxiliaries of the Roman army, and who thought along Roman lines. Such were Julius Classicus (who must have been related to the Classicianus of Britain) and Julius Tutor among the Treveri. Julius Sabinus, the Lingonian noble, claimed descent from Julius Caesar on the wrong side of the blanket, for his great-grandmother had been Caesar's mistress when he was in Gaul. What these men conceived was an *imperium Galliarum*, a Romanized Empire of the Gauls. 'Once we hold the passes of the Alps,' they argued, 'it will be for the Gallic peoples themselves to decide the limits of their power.' Such a position was never reached: but the rebellion brought many humiliations to the Romans.

Civilis captured the great double fortress of Vetera (Xanten), base of the XVth and Vth Legions. After the capture of Novaesium (Neuss) by Classicus the Roman forces took the oath of allegiance to the Empire of the Gauls, as did, later, the people of Cologne and the remaining forces in Upper Germany. In the case of Cologne,[28] be it noted, they did so only under compulsion. An earlier request from the 'free' Germans they had rejected, arguing that Roman colonists and natives now made one '*patria*'. A striking contrast, this, to Camulodunum, founded at the same time. But, even at this crisis, there was effective support in Gaul for the Roman connexion. It was led by the powerful *civitas* of the Remi, at whose instigation a *concilium*[29] was held at Reims to debate the great choice before them—independence or the *pax Romana* (*libertas an pax?*). The *concilium* was, of course, a purely Gallic affair, but its outcome was in favour of Rome. Valentinus, of the Treveri, spoke with wild eloquence in favour of war; 'in a carefully prepared speech he brought out all the charges usually made against great empires, and hurled insults on the Roman people'. More soberly, Julius Auspex, a noble of the Remi, spoke of the power of Rome, and the blessings of peace. In the end, says Tacitus, the assembly praised the spirit of Valentinus, but followed the advice of Auspex. He notes with savage irony how tribal jealousies hindered the war-party of the Gauls from common action: they could not agree upon who should be the war-leader (unlike the Britons with Boudicca!): even before they had won the war, they were quarrelling about where their future capital should be. Among the pro-Roman party a common purpose was to be found, and letters were sent to the Treveri and Lingones, bidding them lay down their arms, and offering to plead their cause. Valentinus was powerful enough with his own people to secure their rejection.

Cerialis tore through this atmosphere of intrigue and disgrace like a strong wind. He dismissed the forces which the loyal Gallic states sent to his assistance; the legions were tools and with them he would finish the job. 'Once Rome starts a war,' he told them, 'it is as good as won.' He led his men on a three-day march to Rigodulum (Riol), where Valentinus and a large force of the Treveri held a strongly fortified hill.[30] This he captured in an engagement which recalls Ostorius Scapula's defeat of Caratacus: the next day he entered Trèves. His troops wanted to sack the place, but he forbade it: instead he summoned an assembly of the Treveri and Lingones, and spoke to them for their own good.

The speech which Tacitus makes him deliver[31] is the most

eloquent defence of Roman imperialism in literature. Nor must we take the views there expressed as the private convictions of Cerialis only; they were those of all provincial governors of the better type. As such, they deserve close analysis. Cerialis began by reminding his audience of the greatest service Rome had rendered Gaul—protection against the Germans from the time of the Cimbri and Teutones, and that of Ariovistus, to the present day. 'The Germans always have the same object in crossing over into Gaul, lust, avarice, and the desire to make themselves masters of your fertile soil . . . of course they talk of freedom and other specious pretexts. . . .' Left to themselves, the Gauls had wars and kingdoms, now they had the Roman army and peace. But peace has its price: 'you cannot have an army without pay, nor pay without taxes'. Moreover (and here his argument is less plausible), Romans and Gauls had everything in common: 'you command our legions, you rule other provinces . . . *nihil separatum clausumve*' (there are no reserved positions, no segregation. Good emperors benefited Gaul as much as Rome. Bad ones should be endured like natural calamities 'such as bad seasons or excessive rains', in the knowledge that they will pass. 'The good fortune and discipline of eight hundred years have built the framework of this empire, which will overwhelm its destroyers if it is destroyed. You stand in the greatest danger, who have gold and wealth, the principal causes of war. So, cherish and love peace and the city of Rome which we both, conquerors and conquered, possess with equal rights. Take heed of the lessons of good and bad fortune; do not choose defiance and ruin rather than obedience and prosperity. . . .' The Treveri were in no position to put questions to their distinguished lecturer, otherwise they might fairly have asked whether—setting aside weather control for the time being— something might not be done to ensure a more regular supply of good emperors, itself the best guarantee of good subordinates. This was indeed the cardinal problem of the Roman Empire, and the system of adoption in force after the death of Nerva gave four good emperors in succession from A.D. 98 to 180, and made possible the 'golden age' of the Roman world. But, apart from complacency on this issue and that of the sharing of privileges, the sentiments of Cerialis are enlightened, even noble. So might have spoken a Vespasian, a Trajan, or a Hadrian.

Having brought down the Empire of the Gauls, Cerialis turned to the second part of his invasion, the reduction of Civilis. This was a longer task, and for the last stages we lack the guidance of Tacitus. We need not follow further, save to note that it was accomplished, and that the XIVth Legion again played a major part in the Roman victory.

Less than ten years separated the rebellion of Boudicca and that of Civilis, the greatest disturbances of the century in the western provinces. They had exposed grave weaknesses in the imperial system, but at least the lessons they taught were well learned. Great care was taken over the selection of governors for these important provinces; emperors studied their problems at first hand. We hear of no more nationalist, separatist movements until the troubled times of the third century brought the "empires" of Postumus in Gaul and Carausius in Britain. Both arose from the weakness of the central power, both collapsed when it was re-established. The general prosperity of the late first and the second century in Britain and Gaul anchored the loyalty of the provincials to Rome.

Thus Cerialis' hopes for the future of Gaul were fulfilled. He still had service to perform in Britain. His military distinction, knowledge of the province, and his personal qualities, made him the ideal choice as the first Flavian governor. With him went the II *Adiutrix*, which had served with him on the Rhine. A new forward policy was planned; circumstances dictated that it should begin in the north, against the Brigantes. The Brigantian problem, it may well be, called for his whole attention in Britain. At any rate, nothing is said of his civil administration.[32] His advance met with stiff opposition—the storming of the great fortified position at Stanwick must have been one such instance—but he pacified the whole territory at least as far as the Tyne-Solway line, and may well have reached that of the Forth-Clyde. These campaigns, and the move forward of the legionary base from Lincoln to York, complete the first phase of the Roman advance to the north. It was now time to take up the problem of Wales, but this was entrusted to Julius Frontinus, who had no previous experience of Britain.

With Julius Agricola, the third Flavian governor, we find a British expert employed for the final stages in Wales and the north, and the last great advance to Caledonia. No previous governor had known so much of Britain and its peoples. Did the experience of the young man who had served on Suetonius's staff leave any mark on the governor who saw it as his mission to 'crown the work of fifty years' in Britain?[33] He had at least learned the lesson, never grasped by Suetonius, that 'military victories count for little, if injustice follows them' (*parum profici armis, si iniuriae sequerentur*). Hence the first winter of his administration was devoted to reforms in the administration: abuses were checked, care taken over appointments and promotions. 'As a result, he brought peace into good repute: the neglect or arrogance of his predecessors had caused it to be dreaded as greatly as war.' Tacitus's comment is here less than just to Petronius Turpilianus and Trebellius Maximus. The second winter was devoted to the *saluberrima consilia* of the drive for Romanization. In the picture of Agricola drawn by Tacitus, the virtues of the civil administrator are combined with those of military expert. Whether we accept this as a true picture or not, we must agree that these were the qualities required in so warlike a province.[34] And, noting the succession of able governors, from the aftermath of the Boudicca rebellion to the reign of Hadrian and beyond, it would seem that this was well understood by the Imperial Government.

6

ARCHAEOLOGY AND THE
REBELLION

THE PAGES OF TACITUS AND DIO reveal the unfolding of a
dreadful story with its dire consequences. We may wonder
whether some of its horrors are not the product of the historians'
imagination. What further evidence in hard unyielding archaeological terms can be found to support the historical narrative?
Earlier antiquaries had little difficulty. In the City of London
the hideous contents of every seventeenth-century plague pit
could be fancifully turned into the victims of Boudicca by
antiquaries steeped in classical learning, just as Kentish earth-
works were linked with Caesar and stone circles with the Druids.
We need today a more solid basis of fact. Archaeological excavation has over the last few decades become a very precise
operation, carried out with the delicate skill of a surgeon and
interpreted with the stiff logic of a scientist. Skeletal remains
need to be in their association with datable material before
being admitted as possible victims of a massacre, while a careful
study of the fragments is necessary to see how death was effected.
When put to these tests, few of the romantic interpretations of
these remains can be substantiated, and it seems unlikely that
a large number of bodies would have been left in the ruins of
sacked towns. One of the first tasks of the Roman authorities
after the event would have been to collect these remains, and
see that they were all properly cremated and buried in the
cemetery areas. Although, as we shall see, there are ample signs
of destruction at Colchester and Verulamium, in neither case

have any human remains been found belonging to this period in the devastated area. The same may be true of London.

There is only one such gruesome example which has been brought forward in modern times. This is from the first-century Roman fort on the Fosse Way at Margidunum, near Nottingham. Dr. Felix Oswald, excavating there between 1910 and 1936, found two pits containing three skeletons, a boy of about 16, a man and a woman.[1] The burial pits also contained a quantity of charcoal and burnt daub indicative of a nearby fire, and although not directly proved, the period is certainly post-Claudian. Examination of the bones showed that all three bodies must have been in an advanced state of decomposition when buried, the head of the woman, for example, being carefully reversed. Furthermore, the sacrum of the man was missing, and this was suggested by Dr. Oswald as evidence that the body had been partly eaten by wolves, and the remains hastily buried when the site was tidied up after the insurrection. This discovery may possibly be associated with the events of A.D. 60. But the dating evidence is incomplete, and the victims may have been unfortunate locals living in the civil settlement of the fort. Presumably, having sought the shelter of the Roman army, they were deemed to be pro-Roman by the rebels. There is too much speculation in this example and not enough reliable evidence.

When we come to the problems of destruction which we know resulted from the revolt, at least at London, Colchester, and Verulamium (St. Albans), we are on surer ground. Even here, however, one needs caution. Excavators have in the past tended to link any signs of burning with some holocaust for which there seemed to be historical warrant. An example of this is the end of the period of Roman occupation, which has tended, in the hands of earlier excavators, to be lost in the smoke of burning towns and villas following the great barbarian conspiracy of A.D. 367. There is a growing amount of archaeological evidence which is throwing doubt on this. We need not merely traces of burning here and there, but whole devastated areas, to support us in following in the track of Boudicca's men. This, coupled with datable pottery and coins in the destruction deposit, would give us a foundation to our story.

From London there comes evidence of two extensive fires in the Roman period. Mr. G. C. Dunning, who has studied them,[2] was able to distinguish them by the burnt pottery, in particular the red glossy samian ware which turns black when subjected to intense heat. Near Lombard Street the burnt layer was found to be 2 ft. thick and bright red in colour, due to the burnt clay and daub from the timber houses. The site of Lloyds Bank produced at a depth of 15 ft. seventeen burnt bronze coins of Claudius. In some cases the heat of the fire has scorched the natural brick earth on which these early houses were standing, reducing it in parts to powder. By plotting on a map of London the examples of the first-century destruction, some idea can be gained of the extent of the Roman city at the time of the revolt, and this agrees with a distribution map of finds of first-century pottery. The centre of the area is on the hill slope north of London Bridge. There is an extension across the Walbrook to the west, probably following a road directed towards what later became the Newgate. Under this medieval structure parts of the original Roman gate have been found.[3] The Roman defences of London are now known to belong to a much later period, but this road was evidently the main way to the west and north,[4] and some ribbon development had spread along it by A.D. 60.

In London it has always been difficult to obtain a clear picture of the Roman occupation, as it is buried so deeply below heavy modern foundations. Elsewhere there are often still these difficulties, but on a smaller scale. Colchester has yielded a wide variety of evidence. At least five instances are recorded of the discovery of burnt buildings with finds which associated them quite certainly with the destruction of A.D. 60. The most dramatic of these occurred when a new café was being built in 1927. Workmen found a seam of Roman pottery and glass which, as Mr. Hull has written, was 'so loose that fragments fell out in a tinkling shower when touched'.[5] When the pieces had been collected and examined, it was seen that they had all been subject to heat and that the range of pottery was very limited. Also it seemed clear that the pots had been carefully stacked at the time of the fire, and above them had been shelves of fine glass, which had melted and dripped on to the pottery. Among the sherds were those of a rhyton, a very rare type of drinking-jug in the form of a human face. These remains belonged to a pottery and glass shop set up in the *colonia* for the early settlers. The date of the pottery and glass fits the sack of A.D. 60 very well, and incidentally gives us a fine range of closely dated types which are of considerable use to excavators elsewhere.[6] Another collection of the same date, including over 350 pieces of plain and seventy decorated samian, came from the extension of a cellar in the High Street next to the Red Lion, and must likewise have come from a shop.[7] When the telephone exchange was built in 1926–9 an archaeological investigation was not possible, but among the casual finds which reached the Museum was a small hoard of twenty-seven burnt coins of Agrippa and Claudius[8] which may have been hidden during the scare preceding the revolt. Clear evidence of destruction also comes from No. 60 North Hill,[9] where a mixed burnt deposit 18 in. thick included baked blocks of clay from the early buildings, and also from the site of St. Nicholas Church.[10]

In the Tacitean account the final stages of the desperate resistance of the veterans came in the Temple of Claudius, which the Britons finally burnt over their heads. This building has been identified and parts of the foundation can be seen today, embedded in the great Norman castle. The temple was rebuilt after the revolt and remained the focus of the imperial cult in the province. The raised platform and the masses of ruined masonry must have been a great attraction to the Normans. It was for them a ready foundation and a source of materials for their castle. So for centuries the great temple remained unknown and forgotten, and might never have been found to this day had it not been for an attempt in 1683 to demolish the Norman castle. A local ironmonger, John Wheely, undertook this work, and in his endeavours to undermine the whole building drove a tunnel through the base of the structure The wall was found to be 25 ft. thick, and inside there were structures having the appearance of vaults. The massive nature of the building made its demolition an arduous and unprofitable business, so Wheely abandoned his efforts after causing considerable devastation to the upper parts of the castle. His tunnel, in providing a section through the wall, enables a close study to be made. Even so, it was not until Sir Mortimer Wheeler and P. J. Laver began a systematic survey of Roman Colchester at the time of the First World War that the full significance of the structure revealed by Wheely's tunnel was appreciated.[11] There were, in fact, two different walls, the outer Norman work only encased the earlier Roman work, and a clear vertical joint can be seen between the construction of the two periods.[12] One can today still pass through Wheely's tunnel into the so-called vaults, to stand below the foundations of the Roman temple. The platform or *podium* was built of a mass of concrete placed on timber shuttering, constructed in the form of a barrel-vault. But there was never any entrance to this part, so it could never have been the temple treasure house (or store) as people have in the past believed. It is simply a method of construction which has left a space below the arched foundation, much enlarged no doubt by Wheely, whose tunnel was partly cut to give access to carts taking away the sand. The ironmonger may have been inspired by the thought of finding a rich treasure hoard in such a place. At least he made possible the discovery and investigation of this remarkable Roman foundation, the only example of a classical type so far discovered in Britain. (Pl. VII.) A close parallel is the still-surviving Maison Carrée at Nîmes.

The Normans have removed all the superstructure at Colchester and with it evidence of the devastation of A.D. 60 and the subsequent rebuilding. One has to look elsewhere for traces of these events. The temple is known to stand in the middle of a large precinct, 535 ft. by 425 ft., but at present very little is known about the internal arrangements. In 1953 there was a limited opportunity, during the rebuilding of some shops, to investigate the south side and main entrance. The remains here were found to be very complex and of a monumental character.[13] It is a very serious reflection on the national attitude towards our antiquities that so recently it was not possible to carry out a full-scale excavation on this part of the most important building in Roman Britain. In front of these remains, running along the edge of the street, a drain was found, and this humble structure produced dramatic evidence of the revolt. The drain, of rather poor construction, designed to take away rainwater from the street, had been made of blocks of alabaster! The stones had at some previous stage been subject to great heat and were, of course, being re-used. The conclusions of the excavator are: 'The drain was built of re-used material and I attribute the decay of the alabaster to the action of fire. The whole could have been salvaged from the ruins of the temple after its destruction by Boudicca and one can imagine that this drain might have been built in this comparatively shoddy manner in a rehabilitation scheme carried out at great speed.' This modest excavation also produced over 200 fragments of marble slabs, and the geological report on these reads like a Cook's tour of the Mediterranean: Africano from Asia Minor, Rosso Antico from Cape Matapan, Pavonazzetto from Phrygia, Giallo Antico from Algeria, Cipollino from Euboea, Carrara from Italy, Porphyry from Greece, and so on. They do not all necessarily belong to the first temple, but show the expense to which the authorities were prepared to go in decorating this building in a fitting style.

To the north-west of the Roman *colonia*, on the ground sloping down to the River Colne, lies Camulodunum, the site of the British settlement. Here King Cunobelinus kept his court, minted his vast numbers of coins, and ruled the greater part of southern England. This was the enemy capital entered by Claudius himself at the head of his army in A.D. 43, and here he received the submission of the eleven British kings. The series of excavations from 1930 to 1939[14] were in some way disappointing, for they produced very little evidence of the type of buildings which must have stood there, but the contribution to the history of the first century is of the greatest importance. The site was used by the Roman Army, and later by the builders of the *colonia*, so there was continuous occupation from pre-Roman times through to A.D. 60. Over almost the whole of the site there were signs of violent destruction, but that was by no means the whole story. Mixed with the debris in several places were lumps of slag and innumerable chippings of sheet bronze and other metal fragments. With these were also found pieces of military equipment and weapons. Evidence pointed to Roman military metalworking on a large scale.

While the occupation at this period has no military character, 'when the destruction took place the military metalworking was evidently at its height. It is a fair conclusion that this intensive activity by Roman armourers belongs to the eve of the destruction and should be connected with it historically: if the rebels were to be resisted at all, there had to be rearmament and rearmament in a hurry. And this is exactly what excavations appear to reveal. The manufacture of new and the repair of old armour and weapons, extemporized in feverish haste on the greatest scale possible in a short time, will account as no other explanation can for these phenomenal findings.'[15] One can well imagine the hectic attempts of the settlers to equip themselves in the face of the sudden emergency. The equipment includes a whole sackful of helmets, pieces of shields, many pieces of iron and buckles from the body armour (*lorica segmentata*), together with many other items associated with both infantry and cavalry.

Of the Britons themselves there was little trace, but 'near the west entrance were three bronze terrets and two bronze and iron linch pins which must stylistically be British work of just this period. Thus, appropriately enough, the only relics they have left us are from the chariots and the horses in which they put their trust.'[16] Appropriate indeed, for of Celtic loan-words in Latin, the longest list is of those dealing with horses and horse-drawn vehicles.

By one of those strange ironies of history, the savage destruction which engulfed Colchester actually preserved monuments in three instances. When the rebels swept down on to the Roman town they found just outside by the roadway a small cemetery with a few upstanding tombstones. These they defaced and pushed over. In the later clearing up, this little area was overlooked and there two of the stones continued to lie, to become overgrown and eventually lost to view. Eventually the two stones were found and can now be seen in the Castle Museum (Pls. V and VI).[17] They are without doubt two of the finest examples of their kind in this country and show the soldiers in their full parade uniform. One belongs to M. Favonius Facilis, a centurion of the XXth Legion. He has lost his nose, but his grim visage is clear enough, and while his left hand fingers the knob of his sword pommel, his right holds the vine stick of his office. The condition of both stones is remarkably good and they could not have stood long in the little cemetery. They had been covered with gesso and painted in naturalistic colours, but only the faintest traces of this remains behind the ears of Facilis. The stone is the finest product of the Bath area, and it says much for the military organization that the army had sought out and started quarrying so early some of the finest stone for monumental masonry in Britain. The second stone is an auxiliary who bears the name Longinus Sdapezematygus, a *duplicarius* of the first *Ala* of Thracians from the district of Sardica.[18] He came from the province of Moesia, which may have been part of Thrace, and his name is a strange mixture of the barbarous and classical. He is portrayed riding his horse over the prostrate foe, a typical theme. The poor naked barbarian with his wild locks and beard crouches in terror under the horse. Longinus has unfortunately lost the whole of his face, which has been smashed off by a heavy blow before the stone was turned over, but the details of his scale armour and the decorative trappings on his horse are very sharp. These two stones belong to serving soldiers and not veterans from the *colonia*; they must have been erected during the time of Aulus Plautius, the first governor of Britain, when Camulodunum was the main military base and where presumably the XXth Legion was held in reserve with some auxiliary units.

The third object which Fate has preserved is a bronze head thought to be that of the Emperor Claudius (Pl. VIII). It was found in 1907 in the River Alde at Rendham, near Saxmundham, Suffolk.[19] The head is life size and the jagged edge round the neck shows that it was ruthlessly hacked away from its body. Since the time of Sir George Macdonald the view has been held that this bronze head must have been part of the loot carried away from Colchester after the devastation. Later, when the Roman Army began its campaign of terror in East Anglia, a piece like this would have become too hot to hold, and one can imagine its once proud possessor in a moment of panic pitching it into the river, where it remained until an inquisitive little boy fished it out in 1907. Sir George Macdonald boldly postulated that it was the head from the actual cult statue in the temple, but, as Professor Toynbee has suggested, it would in that case have been more than life size and the workmanship of a better quality. 'It is more likely', she writes, 'to have adorned some other public building, such as the theatre or the basilica. The slight backward tilt of the head *may* mean, as was once suggested,[20] that we have here the remnant of an equestrian statue; at any rate, it must have stood at some height above ground-level, since the eyes gaze out into the distance, as though above the heads of, and oblivious of, bystanders.'

A cache of loot was found in 1962 near Hockwold Fen by an ancient road. It consisted of five silver cups from which feet and handles had been forcibly removed before burial. Three of the cups are skilfully decorated in relief and incised work, probably from an Italian workshop and datable to *c.* 100 B.C. to A.D. 50. Silver objects of this kind are likely to have remained in use or as family possessions for a considerable time, although some of them may have been antique by A.D. 60. While there may have been an earlier event, the revolt would seem to be a good historical context for their seizure as loot and burial before retribution overtook their unlawful owner.

The site of the Roman town of Verulamium, the tribal centre of the Catuvellauni, has been preserved for us by the martyrdom of St. Alban. After his sentence had been passed, presumably in the Forum, he would have been led to a place of execution across the River Ver to a higher place on the other side of the valley. It was here, a spot hallowed by tradition, that the monks built St. Alban's Abbey and round which the modern town has grown and developed, while the ruins of the Roman town crumbled and were covered with vegetation. Several opportunities have been taken in modern times of exploring Verulamium. The first large-scale attempt was made by Sir Mortimer Wheeler in 1930 and the years following.[21] At several points evidence of destruction in A.D. 60 was encountered, but the presence of later Roman buildings prevented the stripping of large areas to explore the earlier levels. It is clear that this excavation was on the edge of the early town. Evidence of a more positive and dramatic quality has been forthcoming in the more recent excavations by Mr. S. S. Frere. This investigation was started in 1955, in advance of the widening of Blue

House Hill, a modern lane which follows one of the more important Roman streets through the centre of the town. It was not until 1957 that Mr. Frere was able to begin a systematic study of the first-century levels. The black layer of charcoal and burnt timbers contrasted strongly against the bright red of the burnt clay and daub, and the story of the revolt stood out in bright technicolour. (Pl. X.) At one point these layers were found to be sandwiched between structures, the interpretation of which has a close bearing on our story. This occurred on the north side of the town just above the flood plain of the River Ver, where Mr. Frere was looking for the defences in 1956.[22] A section was cut at right-angles to the alignment and the footings and base of the town wall were found, together with its bank. It had been shown in 1955 that these defences, like those of other towns of Roman Britain, belong to the end of the second century.[23] Below these defences were the remains of an earlier system of quite different character, consisting of a turf and timber revetted bank typical of military construction. This lay immediately over a scatter of pre-Roman occupation, and it seems likely that we have here the defences of a fort of a Roman unit, soon after A.D. 43. One must appreciate here that the Catuvellauni were the main opponents of the Romans at this time in Britain, although the branch here may have differed in its political affinities. This area of Verulamium has produced a small collection of military equipment which fits this sequence very well. In the tail of the early bank sandwiched between these two defences were the remains of two houses. The earliest of these must have been built soon after the army moved out, and it was this timber dwelling which was destroyed by the rebels and which showed up as a mass of red daub and black ash. Above this deposit had accumulated over a considerable time some material washed down from the back, and on this again was the second house which in turn was sealed by the late second-century bank. Thus in one short section much of the history of Verulamium was epitomized, though it was demonstrated only through the skilled and discerning eye of Mr. Frere. In Insula XIV a block of shops had been destroyed but rebuilt in much the same manner, suggesting that the owner survived and was able to reinstate himself after the revolt.

Although the greater part of the IXth Legion was ambushed and annihilated in the field, a garrison would have been left at the fortress at Lincoln, and there is nothing in the account to suggest that this was also captured. The commander Cerialis escaped from the battle and with his horsemen reached the safety of his headquarters. When the legionary defences were first discovered and investigated in 1941–2,[24] one of the most interesting features was a tower projecting from the front of the rampart. It was not part of the original scheme, but an addition to the defences, and it was necessary to fill in the innermost ditch. The conclusion one could reasonably draw from this is that the tower was constructed in order to strengthen the defences of the fortress. Projecting towers are very unusual at this period and might be said to anticipate the defensive architecture of the fourth century, when large stone bastions became the accepted practice. It might therefore be argued that Cerialis felt very insecure and it would be interesting to connect this reconstruction with the revolt. If the legion was now much reduced and the whole of the Roman forces in Britain in jeopardy, Cerialis might well feel the need at Lincoln for extra stiff defences against the victorious rebels. Artillery and archers were able to command the front of the walls or rampart and deal with any threat of serious siege-work.

The same attempt at stiffening the defences may have occurred at the fort at Great Casterton, Rutland.[25] Here the Claudian fort had in a subsequent stage of its history been reduced in size. It was the south ditch of this reduced fort which was deepened from 5 to 8 ft. and widened from 14 to 18 ft. The abnormal size of the new ditch hewn out of the bed rock reflects a serious threat to the garrison at or about this time, but there is at present no precise dating evidence to link it with the revolt.

As work progresses on the Roman military sites of the Midlands, especially those along Watling Street, more evidence of this great drama will appear. There is a hint that the large 26-acre fort at Kinvaston, in South Staffordshire, may have held the rearguard of the main advance force[25a] but more work is needed here before the full story is understood. The same is true of Letocetum (Wall, near Lichfield) where traces of at least three military forts have been encountered, while near Coventry a small fort has produced coins of Nero.[25b] In this area, there must be reflected in the shape of military camps, forts, signal stations, store bases, etc., the waves of advance and withdrawal. First the advance under Scapula, then consolidation and holding units gradually being drawn forward as the offensive into Wales intensified. The revolt meant not only strengthening of defences, but the army on the move again, backwards and forwards. We have come to expect the unravelling of the complicated histories of northern forts in such skilled hands as Professor I. A. Richmond. Now it will be for others to come to grips with similar problems on these Midland sites. But it will demand much careful and large-scale excavation before the truth will be known in detail.

Apart from the site of the final battle itself, the most dramatic discovery would be that of the sacred groves of the Druids' sanctuary, which were destroyed by the Roman troops. This event is unfortunately unlikely, as there would be little archaeological trace of such a site. The nearest approach was the discovery of the Llyn Cerrig Bach hoard of ironwork. During the construction of the Royal Air Force Station at Valley, in the last war, peat was required, and this was taken out of a nearby bog and spread about the station. While this work was being carried out sundry iron objects were found and left on the site. One substantial chain was in fact used by a tractor for hauling lorries which had stuck in the soft mud. In 1943 no one could be blamed for having his mind on other matters, and it took time for the antiquity of these objects to be recognized and for them to be collected together, treated and studied. It is very fortunate that so many as 143 separate objects were recovered,[26] and also that they were so promptly published under wartime conditions by Sir Cyril Fox, who was at the time Director of the National Museum of Wales.[27] The objects are mostly of iron, but there are also bronzes and a few fragments of wood preserved by the peat. The variety is also considerable, but most of the objects are military. Parts of eleven swords, three scabbards and seven spears are listed, a number of fragments of war chariots and much harness gear. Objects of outstanding interest are two gang chains, one of which with five neck rings is complete, and part of a bronze trumpet. A few items are of high artistic merit. As Sir Cyril Fox has indicated, the collection has a remarkable homogeneity, every single object belongs to the late Iron Age and there is no Roman influence. He was also able to demonstrate that the deposit was drawn from widely different cultural contexts which range over the greater part of England from the Brigantes of Yorkshire to the Dumnonii of the south-west, although nothing can be directly attributed to the Iceni. No pottery was found, but there were bones in plenty, mostly pig, ox, goat, and sheep.

A feature noticed when the objects were cleaned is that most of them had been deliberately broken or damaged in a manner very similar to the hoards from the Danish peat bogs. It is known from accounts by Posidonius that it was a Celtic practice to collect together the spoils of war and deposit them in sacred places including lakes and pools.[28] The conclusion, then, which can be drawn from the study of this rich hoard is that this is one of these sacred deposits. The spoils of war or tribute drawn from most of the Celtic tribes of Britain were ceremonially destroyed and cast into the sacred pool which was originally here. The wealth and variety of the objects indicate a powerful community present in Anglesey at this time and this must surely be that of the Druids. It would, however, be a mistake to assume that the hoard represents some of the wealth of the Druids thrown away in panic on the approach of the Roman Army. It is much more likely that this sacred pool was the scene of periodic ceremonies when the metalwork and remains of the feastings were cast upon the waters as an offering to the gods.

The aftermath of the revolt was the devastation of the territory of the Iceni, which must have had the same effect as the visitation of William the Conqueror to the Vale of York. One would expect that some archaeological traces would be found in the form of burnt homesteads and slow recovery. So far very little positive evidence has been produced. Here and there coin and bronze hoards of the period may represent the wealth of natives who perished in the débâcle. Nor are there so far any satisfactory indications of Roman military occupation at this time apart from a few objects of equipment from Caistor-next-Norwich and Felixstowe.[29] It might be argued that the map of

Roman Britain shows a much sparser development here than in other parts of England. But this may be equally due to lack of local field work or the presence of the heavy clay lands which lie over much of the area. We need far more detailed knowledge of the development of the towns and countryside before any conclusions can be drawn. Evidence of this nature may come from Hockwold Fen, where the Roman town of Camboritum has been recently identified. It was a site which had to be abandoned at the end of the second century, possibly due to flooding when the Ouse changed its course.

One interesting fact needing consideration is the siting of the tribal centre at Caistor-by-Norwich. The evidence at present points to the western and north-western parts of Norfolk as the main centre of the Iron Age culture and not the area of the Roman town. One might be tempted to suggest that here at least is either a deliberate Roman policy in establishing the capital in a new area or at the centre of a minor branch of the tribe, or that the devastation of the more flourishing area may have been so thorough that the process was one of natural selection. The excavator at Caistor, Mr. D. Atkinson, considered that the town was not founded until after the revolt,[30] and its size of fifty acres puts it into a modest class. There are still many difficult problems in the siting of the roads and minor settlements. One place yet to be discovered is Villa Faustini of the Antonine Itinerary. This name suggests the presence of a large estate in the area which may have been state-owned. Appropriation of the best lands and enslavement of the population would have been the natural outcome of the revolt and the devastation would have left permanent scars on East Anglia during the Roman period. Careful field work and excavation will undoubtedly in time help to fill the sad gaps in our story.

BOUDICCA IN HISTORY AND TRADITION

THERE IS SOMETHING yet to be added to the account of the Boudicca rebellion and its aftermath. In the noble epilogue to the *Agricola* Tacitus holds out to the bereaved family the consolation that 'oblivion has overtaken many of the ancients, as though they had been without glory or distinction. But Agricola's story has been recounted and entrusted to posterity; and he will live.'[1] This service, which in the *Agricola* he saw as the supreme act of *pietas* to his father-in-law, he has, of course, performed for all the other characters in his historical work. But the immortality thus attained in the record of history is no static condition: it is no less at the mercy of time and chance than life on earth. Our last task, then, is to give a sketch—more than that it cannot be—of the treatment of Boudicca in British history and tradition.

We may begin with Gildas, and that remarkable work *De Excidio Britanniae*, where Boudicca gets a most unfavourable notice. She is 'that deceitful lioness, who put to death the rulers they (the Romans) had left in Britain, to unfold more fully and to complete the enterprise of the Romans. When the news reached the Senate, they at once sent an army to take vengeance on the crafty foxes, as they called them. But there was no navy on the seas . . . no army mustered on land . . . the Britons' backs were their shields, they offered their necks to the sword, and stretched out their hands, like women, to be bound. So that it has become a proverb that the Britons are neither bold in war nor faithful in peace.'[2] A disastrous affair in every way, it would seem: it should never have been undertaken, but once undertaken it should have been better managed. That has been said, subsequently, of other British ventures. In Gildas, of course, we have the last voice that speaks for Roman Britain, belabouring all who contributed to the ruin of the province. For him 'rebellion against Rome is an ungrateful sin';[3] his hostility to the new native 'tyrants' who had hacked their way to power over the ruins of the imperial order would prejudice him against earlier champions of British independence. Bede, like Nennius, has a reference to the rebellion, but not to Boudicca herself. 'Nero succeeded Claudius in the Empire, but undertook nothing whatever in military enterprise. So, among countless other disasters to the Roman rule, he almost lost Britain: for in his time two very noble cities were captured and destroyed.'[4] The source here is Suetonius. Tacitus, by now, has been virtually lost, and with him has gone all memory of Boudicca.

It would seem that there are no Welsh traditions about her, and she has no part in that Welsh version of British history that took shape in the early Middle Ages. Indeed, it is easy to see that, even if she had been known, she would scarcely do. There were no women rulers in early Wales: membership of the *cenedl* descended through the male line: daughters could not even inherit land. A British Queen would be most unedifying. So, too, would a rebel against Rome, for the Welsh were passionately interested in the Trojan ancestry of the British, through Brutus, and that would make them cousins of the descendants of Aeneas. To establish this was one great task of Welsh historiography. The others were to trace the coming of Christianity to Britain (the Glastonbury story, King Lucius, etc.), and to narrate the deeds of the British champions in the struggle against the Saxons.

All these ingredients were assembled and used in that wonderful concoction, the *Historia Regum Britanniae* of Geoffrey of Monmouth. Here, *posteritati narratus et traditus*, is the landing of Brutus, Diana's prophecy of a British Empire, the long line of kings of Britain, with Lear and Bladud, and Brennus who conquered Gaul and Rome, and Cassibellaunus, who twice defeated Julius Caesar. Then there is Arviragus—a name picked up out of Juvenal—who submitted to Claudius, and married the Emperor's daughter; Lucius, who was converted to Christianity about A.D. 150; Coel, father of Helen, the mother of the Emperor Constantine. Here, too, in its perfected form, is the figure of Arthur, of Roman descent, who defeats the Saxons, builds a northern Empire, conquers Gaul, and is re-called by civil war when about to march on Rome itself. From his last battle he is borne away wounded to Avalon, from whence . . . The work of Geoffrey of Monmouth is one of the supreme examples of manipulated history. Had he known of Boudicca, she would have been very serviceable. A recent study[5] has pointed out the high importance of his women sovereigns, Gwendolena, Cordelia, Helena; above all, the noble and liberal Marcia, the great law-giver. All this, of course, in the interest of the Empress Matilda and her claims to sovereignty in England. Boudicca would have been a precedent lying very ready to his hand. But the rediscovery of Tacitus was yet to come.

About 1360 Boccaccio paid his famous visit to the library of the monastery of Monte Cassino, which he found in a ruinous and neglected condition. Among the manuscripts which he claims to have 'rescued' was one of Tacitus, though it is un-certain which. From this begins the Tacitean corpus, as we now have it. *Annals* i–iv are contained in the First Medici manuscript, discovered about 1410; xi–xvi and *Histories* i–v in the Second, found about 1430. The hunt for other manuscripts of Tacitus was one of the main concerns of the Italian scholars of the early fifteenth century. Printed editions came in the second half of that century: the *editio princeps*, of the younger Spira, appearing at Venice about 1470. New material was introduced by Beroaldus in the edition he made for Pope Leo X in 1515, and a major landmark in Tacitus studies is marked by the great scholarly edition of the whole corpus by Rhenanus in 1533. From the end of the fifteenth century Tacitus had a deep influence on the historical and political thought of Renaissance Europe.

For the history of Roman Britain, its results are first effec-tively displayed in the famous *Anglica Historia* of Polydore Vergil, the manuscript of which was written in 1512–13, while the first printed edition appeared at Basle in 1534. Armed with the full battery of continental scholarship, which included not only the *Agricola* and *Annals* of Tacitus but also the *Epitome* of Dio Cassius and Suetonius, Polydore Vergil was able to hole the legendary British History[6] below the waterline, although that leaky old vessel sailed on until well into the seventeenth century. Polydore Vergil is often praised for the cool scepticism with which he treats the Trojan kings of Britain and the exploits of Arthur; a scepticism which drew furious retort from the patriotic British historians. This is fair. But his incursions into the topography of Roman Britain lead to conclusions worthy of the most muddle-headed of native antiquaries. He argues soundly, though, that the name of London was not Trinobantum: the Trinobantes he says lived in Essex, and their chief city was Colchester. But then there is the name Ordovicum, which he takes to be the name of a city, and, with the addition of the letter N, to be identified with Norwich. More notorious is his confusion, through the common use of Mona, of Anglesey and the Isle of Man. This credits Suetonius Paulinus with a Manx campaign, and this *drang nach norden* is startlingly apparent in his account of the Boudicca rebellion, which he treats at length. He is first led astray by Ptolemy's mention of a northern Camulodunum, which he takes to be the *colonia*, and places at either Doncaster or Pontefract, 'where there are still extant signs and remains of a temple dedicated to Claudius Caesar'.[7] Some strange results follow. Caratacus becomes 'a powerful ruler among the inhabitants of the Cheviot hills'. The Iceni have to be split into two: the first, who were concerned in the rebellion against Ostorius Scapula in 48, are placed between the Severn and the Wye; the second, called distinctively the Igeni, who inhabit Northumberland. Their king was Prasutagus; his wife Voadicia was 'bannished by the old veterans, her daughters outraged etc.' Then (and here the narrative gets really confused, even in its own terms), Voadicia is appointed leader, the Trinobantes slide away from their allegiance. Where the war is conducted, we are never sure: the veterans are killed 'in a certain temple' (? in the northern Camulodunum, or the southern?): the army of 'Petus Cerialis' is defeated: Suetonius appears in London and quickly leaves it, but we are not told that Voadicia captures it. She does, however, capture Verulamium ('Warlingcester, opposite the village called St. Albans'), fights an unsuccessful battle, and takes poison. 'And from that time on the condition of the island was more peaceful.' It is clear from this that Polydore Vergil used Dio, Suetonius, Ptolemy, and Tacitus, but that he failed to compare them or consider discrepancies. Above all, he did not realize that the primary source is Tacitus.

National pride accounts for the even more drastic swing to the north given to all these events by the great Scottish historian, Hector Böece (d. 1536).[8] This extends, indeed, to the whole history of the Roman conquest of Britain. Again, the starting-point is the location of Camulodunum. Identifying this with the Roman fort of Camelon, near Falkirk, he is able to bring Caesar into Scotland in his second campaign. Caratacus becomes a king of the Scots: 'Arviragus' takes over the role of Boudicca's husband: she herself appears as 'Voda': the campaigns are distributed between Voda and a daughter Voadicia. Catus Decianus, Suetonius, and Petilius Cerealis all appear, in their correct order (Boece knew his Tacitus), but in the wrong geographical context. When it is added that Boece recounted the exploits of some forty early kings of Scotland known previously only by name, and made Arthur 'promise Britain to the Pictish royal house after his death', it will be obvious that his history was of a kind to warm Scottish hearts. It evoked furious protest from south of the border for the rest of the century.

The abiding work of the great Tudor antiquaries, headed by Leland and Camden, was to place British topography on a sound footing. Kendrick has pointed out that 'the first skeletal map of Roman Britain was produced by the work of Robert Talbot (*c.* 1505–1558) on the Antonine Itinerary'.[9] Camden had a sound general grasp of the tribal areas of Roman Britain, which he used as the basis for the grouping of the counties of England and Wales into regions. His account of the Roman occupation is based on the critical use of the best authorities. Camulodunum, it is true, he does not get right, for he places it at Malden in Essex, but he mentions its capture by 'Boadicea'; while the entry under St. Albans records that 'In the reign of the same Nero, when Bunduica or Boadicia Queen of the Icenes, in her deep love of her country and conceived bitter hatred of the Romans, it (Verulamium) was destroyed by the Britons.'[10] There is no mention of the sack of London. For Camden, the Trojan descent of the Britons still has its appeal. 'I enter of times with this cogitation, that Britons may more truly ingrosse themselves into the Trojan stock, by these Romans who are descended from the Trojans . . . than either the Arverni, Mamertini . . . Aedui, or the rest . . . And meet it is that we, Britons and Romans, have grown into one stock or nation . . . This island hath been named Romania and Insula Romana.'

The times of Queen Elizabeth I were most propitious for the fame of Boudicca. A queen, a patriot, of that British stock from which the Tudors came, she had fought gloriously against the invaders of her country. What more could be asked, except success? Moreover, there was among the Elizabethans a wider historical consciousness towards the past, which disposed them to weave the separate strands of Welsh, English, or Norman tradition into a single greater fabric. It is very apparent in the plays of Shakespeare, whether he is dealing with the history of England or what we should now call the legendary history of Britain. Thus in *Cymbeline*, the Roman wars end in reconstruction

> 'So let a Roman and a British ensign wave
> Friendly together: so through Lud's town[11]
> And in the temple of great Jupiter
> Our peace we'll ratify: seal it with Feasts . . .'

To Shakespeare's audience, there was no doubt that Cymbeline and his Britons were ancestors of theirs. At a much lower level, we find Stephen Gosson in the *School of Abuse* (1579) using Boudicca's speech in Dio Cassius to emphasize the degeneracy of the times.[12]

'Consider with thy selfe (gentle Reader) the olde discipline of Englande, mark what we were before, and what we are now: Leaue Rome a while, and cast thine eye backe to thy Predecessors, and tell mee howe wonderfully wee haue beene chaunged, since wee were schooled with these abuses. Dion sayth, that english men could suffer watching and labor, hunger and thirst, and beare of al stormes with hed and shoulders, they vsed slender weapons, went naked, and were good soldiours, they fed vppon rootes and barkes of trees, they would stand vp to the chin many dayes in marishes without victualles: and they had a kind of sustenaunce in time of neede, of which if they had taken but the quantitie of a beane, or the weight of a pease, they did neyther gape after meate, nor long for the cuppe, a great while after. The men in valure not yeelding to Scithia, the women in courage passing the Amazons. The exercise of both was shootyng and darting, running and wrestling and trying such maisteries, as eyther consisted in swiftnesse of feete, agilitie of body, strength of armes, or Martiall discipline. But the exercise that is nowe among vs, is banqueting, playing, pipyng, and dauncing, and all suche delightes as may win vs to pleasure, or rooke vs a sleepe.

'Oh what a woonderfull chaunge is this? Our wreastling at arms, is turned to wallowyng in Ladies laps, our courage, to cowardice, our running to ryot, our Bowes into Bolles, and our Dartes to Dishes.'

But the sharpest appreciation of the Boudicca story and its contemporary relevance was shown by that remarkable, if minor, figure Petruccio Ubaldini (? 1524–1600).[13] Of Florentine parentage, he came to England in 1545, and entered the service of the Crown. He took part in the Scottish campaigns of 1549, after which he returned to the Continent, to write a report on England for the Signoria at Venice. In 1562 he returned, under the patronage of the Earl of Arundel. His subsequent career shows the true versatility of the Renaissance scholar. He gave Italian lessons at Court, illustrated manuscripts, wrote a life of the Emperor Charles (the first Italian book printed in England), and a *Description of the Kingdom of Scotland*, which was taken from Boece. In 1588 he composed a Sallustian memoir on the defeat of the Armada, and at the end of that year we find him exchanging gifts with the Queen, receiving five-and-a-half ounces of gilt plate, and giving a manuscript. This was, almost certainly, his most important work, the *Vite delle Donne Illustre di Regno dell'Inghilterre e della Scotia*, published as a book in 1591. 'The lives of the Noble Ladies of the Kingdom of England and Scotland'—

there is significance both in the theme and its scope. Already, in 1577, he had written on the lives of women, having dedicated a work on 'Six Famous Ladies' to the Queen. The *Vite delle Donne* was a work on an ampler scale, and of a semi-philosophical nature, containing 'sundry arguments political, moral, and economic'. Biography—witness the success of North's translation of Plutarch's *Lives* published in 1579—was highly esteemed for its didactic value. Ubaldini would show that the lives of his Noble Ladies would serve as well for precept and example as the noble Greeks and Romans. From the Roman and British past, he chooses 'Carthumandua', 'Guindelona' (daughter of Coroneus, who came over with Brutus), and Boudicca, who appears with her double, 'Voadicia—Bunduica' (here the influence is almost certainly that of Boece). Ubaldini is uncertain whether there were two historical figures or one: nor does he think it matters, for the moral is the thing. In fact, his Voadicia is largely drawn from Tacitus, Bunduica from Dio and Boece. Thus the story of Voadicia serves to show that 'Tyranny often produces crimes, which through their outrages give rise to a longing for vengeance, so that all justice is destroyed'. We are then told of the wrongdoings of the Roman officials, unworthy of Roman temperance and justice, and of Voadicia's noble disdain. She displays honourable valour in a long and dangerous war, the final battle of which proves that military discipline (i.e. of the Romans) overcomes all obstacles. Voadicia herself, unwilling to appear in a triumph, perishes by her own hand, 'leaving to posterity the memory of a rare fortitude of mind, and of an honourable and noble prudence'. The Bunduica story is told at greater length, and takes as a text 'that cruelty diminishes all praise for honourable valour, and more in war, than in any other activity'. It touches on the infamous memory of Nero, the greed (*avaritia*) of Seneca, the vendetta waged by Bunduica, the sacking of Camulodunum and Verulamium. Then came her notorious cruelties (*notevole crudeltà*), her military prowess, the Roman victory as an example of the triumph of a small skilled force over a disorderly multitude, and Bunduica's suicide, which frees her from shame and reproach. Waving aside the question whether there was one Bunduica or two, Ubaldini concludes by saying that she 'deserves a place among the Noble Ladies of this realm by her marvellous quality' (*per le sue maravigliose virtu*), and that the cruelties she practised on her enemies must not be allowed to outweigh her many praiseworthy deeds, since she was under a *furor di vendetta*.

Some twenty years after the appearance of Ubaldini's book, the story of Boudicca was presented on the stage in the *Bonduca* of John Fletcher, which was acted by Richard Burbage and the King's Men in 1610.[13] In view of its dramatic qualities, it is perhaps surprising that the theme was not taken up earlier. It is worth remembering that about this time the greatest dramatist of the age was engaged on themes from British antiquity. *King Lear* is dated to 1605–6, and *Cymbeline* to 1609–10; Holinshed's *Chronicles* is regarded as the direct historical source of both plays. Since he also recounts the story of Boudicca, one may fairly speculate what Shakespeare might have done with that theme. But this fancy should be set aside, and we should note with gratitude what was actually done by Fletcher. His *Bonduca*, though it does not seem to find its way into the fashionable anthologies of Elizabethan and Jacobean drama, is still a most readable play.[14] Though it shows a knowledge of Tacitus, Dio, and Ubaldini, Fletcher has not cramped himself by any undue regard for historical veracity. The scene of the play is 'Britain', quite unlocalized: indeed, Mona is the only place-name it contains, though there is a reference to the capture of the 'Roman colonies'. Most interesting is the treatment of Bonduca. Despite its title, she is not the real hero of the play. That role belongs to Caratach,[15] a synthesis of the historical Caratacus and the 'Caractacus, cousin to Voadicia' of Boece and Ubaldini. Gallant, chivalrous, and high-minded—indeed, almost intolerably so—he is the true leader of the British cause. The key to Bonduca's character is given in the list of persons represented, where she is called 'Queen of the Iceni, a bold Virago, by Prosutagus'. The virago of Elizabethan tradition is of course, a woman with manly qualities: those of Bonduca are her courage in battle and the fortitude with which she meets her end: her excessive emotion and insensate thirst for vengeance derive from the worst of (traditional) feminine nature. Above all, it is her folly and impetuosity on the battlefield which turns triumph into disaster for the Britons. As he watches the fatal consequences of her order Caratach turns on her in anguish

> *Car.*   Why do you offer to command? the divell,
>   The divell and his dam too, who bid you
>   Meddle in men's affairs?
> *Bond.* I'll help all.
> *Car.*   Home,
>   Home and spin woman, spin, go spin, ye trifle . . .[16]

What prompted Fletcher to supersede Bonduca with the invented Caratach? Was there, in King James's first years, an anti-feminism, bred of Europe's experience of its earlier monstrous regiment of women? Or no more than the need to provide a good part for Burbage? Perhaps the point cannot be settled. The play is notable for the excellence of its sub-plots. One of these is supplied by the story of Poenius Postumus, his refusal to obey orders, and his suicide. To these historical elements Fletcher adds inventions of his own—that 'Penius' had earlier been commander in Britain, that—like the popular tradition about Owen Glyndwr and the battle of Shrewsbury—he was an onlooker at the defeat of Bonduca—also, that 'Swetonius' would not lose Penius for all Britain. Another is the love of the Roman officer Junius for Bonduca's younger daughter: a love which the young woman exploits in the most skilful fashion to enslave him and his companions, until she is stopped unsympathetically[17] by her uncle Caratach and told to play the game. Several of the minor characters are well drawn. The brave boy Hengo recalls young Macduff, or the princes in the Tower in *King Richard the Third*: Judas and his four Roman soldiers are like Pistol, Nym, and Bardolph. Bonduca's daughters are nicely differentiated: in her hour of trial one is resolute like Antigone, the other weak like Ismene. On the Roman side, Swetonius is a noble and chivalrous figure, fit match for Caratach. While the balance is held fairly between the British and the Roman cause, the moral of the play seems to be that contained in Bonduca's dying words:

> 'If you would keep your Laws and Empire whole[10]
> Place in your *Roman's* flesh a *Britain's* soul'.

Here may be mentioned—though out of place—the two other plays on the Boudicca theme—the verse tragedy *Boadicia, Queen of Britain*, by Richard Hopkins (1697), and the *Boadicia* of Richard Glover, produced in Dublin in 1753.[19] This last is an altogether slighter play than that of Fletcher, to which it owes a good deal. Once again the Icenian queen is deprived of leadership of the British cause in favour of a man, Dumnorix, chief of the Trinobantes, and married to her sister Venusia. Again there is a sub-plot of two Roman prisoners, and their love for the Queen's daughter, Emmeline.

A most interesting treatment of the story of Boudicca is that of John Milton in his *History of Britain*, published in 1670.[20] Though aware of its fabulous elements, he cannot bring himself to discard wholly the Trojan legend . . . 'those old and inborn names of successive kings, never any to have been real persons, or done in their lives at least some part of what hath been so long remembered, cannot be thought without too strict an incredulity'. But with the invasion of Caesar he is conscious of having moved on to firmer ground. The history of Roman Britain he regards as 'a story of much truth, and for the first hundred years and somewhat more, collected without much labour, so many and so prudent were the writers, which those two, the civilest and the wisest of European nations, both Italy and Greece, afforded to the actions of that puissant city'. There follows a long and critical account of the exploits of Julius Caesar, the Claudian invasion, and the Caratacus episode. But, by the time the Boudiccan rebellion is reached, Milton becomes impatient, and out of humour with the classical authorities. So much so, that he breaks off a paraphrase of Boudicca's speech as given by Dio with the remark 'a deal of other fondness they put into her mouth not worth recital: how she was lashed, how her daughters were handled, things worthier silence, retirement, and a vail, than for a woman to repeat, as done to her own person, or to hear repeated before a host of men. . . . And this they (the Greek historians) do out of vanity, hoping to embellish their history with the strangeness of our manners, not caring in the meanwhile to brand us with the rankest note of barbarism, as if in Britain women were men, and men women—I affect not set speeches in a history, unless known for certain to have been so spoken in effect as they are written, nor then, unless with rehearsal; and to invent such, though eloquently, as some historians, raising in them that read other conceptions of these times and persons than were there.' Deplorable as was Boudicca's immodesty in Milton's eyes, her lack of generalship in the last battle was worse— 'Hitherto what we have heard of Cassibelan, Togadumnus, Venusius, and Caractacus, hath been full of magnanimity, soberness, and martial skill; but the truth is, that in this battle and whole business the Britons never more plainly manifested themselves to be right barbarians: no rules, no foresight, no fore-cast, experience, or estimation, either of themselves or of their enemies: such confusion, such impotence, as seemed likest not to a war, but to the wild hurry of a distracted woman, with as mad a crew at her heels.' It will be recalled that Milton, casting round for a subject for epic, had once thought of the story of Arthur, or something else from British antiquity. Clearly the Boudicca theme is not one of those which he might have found congenial.

The list of characters in Fletcher's *Bonduca* includes 'Heralds, Druides, Soldiers'. The Druids do no more than kindle the fire at a sacrifice: they are given a song, but do not prophesy. No such subordinate role was theirs in the speculation of seven-teenth- and eighteenth-century antiquaries. The full story of Druidic theories, culminating in Iolo Morgannwg's inventions of Druidical rites for the Eisteddfod, and in the mystic Albion of Blake's *Jerusalem*, has been told by Sir Thomas Kendrick and Stuart Piggott.[21] It forms one of the oddest chapters of British antiquity, and led, indirectly, to certainly the most *outré* of all theories ever propounded about Boudicca. This is the idea put forward by Edmund Bolton that her tomb was no less than Stonehenge itself—'that STONAGE was a works of the BRITANNS, the rudeness itself proclaims'. This was too much, even for his own time, and the idea found no more accep-tance than his much-canvassed proposal for an 'Academ Royal'.[22]

A very typical seventeenth-century work, alike in its classical learning and its muddle-headedness, is that of Aylett Sammes in his *Britannia Antiqua Restaurata* (1676).[23] A paraphrase of Tacitus and Dio is accompanied by a 'Sculpture of Boadicia' (see Frontispiece) based on the description in Dio, and with a verse caption explaining the moral of her history.

The 'grave of Boadicea' continued to haunt the imagination of eighteenth-century antiquaries, though none of them produced so grandiose an identification—what other was there to produce?—as Stonehenge. But it is to this period which we can trace those 'traditions' which associate her name with various mounds in London and the eastern counties, the tumulus in Parliament Hill Fields, for example; that at Harrow Weald,[24] and at the Bubberies in Essex. When Stukeley and his friends adopted for their 'Society of Roman Knights' the names of various figures from Romano-British history it was not likely that that of Boudicca would be overlooked: it was in fact assumed by Lady Hertford.[25] For the sober side of the eighteenth century we may turn to two books, one a specialist study and the other a standard history. The great *Britannia Romana* of John Horsley, published in 1732, marks the beginning of the study of Roman Britain as we know it. By now the texts of classical authors were in fairly sound condition, and it was possible to assemble all the authorities for a given historical event, to compare, and to evaluate them. We find in Horsley[26] a plain straightforward account of the rising, with no flights of fancy, apart from his suggestion that the final battle took place south of the Thames. His list of inscriptions and other Roman antiquities—one of the most valuable features of his book—contains nothing relevant to Boudicca. But perhaps he, more than anyone else, is responsible for perpetuation of the spelling as 'Boadicea'—'this name', he says, 'is writ very variously, not only in modern, but also in ancient authors. . . . As it (Boadicea) has been stamped with the authority of some good English authors, I hope it may pass the more current.'

David Hume's *History of England* (published in 1776) was very widely read by several generations, and played a great part in shaping their picture of the past of Britain. Again, it is a straightforward and sober account, based largely on Tacitus; it does not mention Camulodunum nor Verulamium, and Londinium is called 'a Roman colony'. Hume is severe on the Druids, seeing in them the 'enthusiasm' which the eighteenth century found so repugnant. 'No idolatrous worship ever attained such an ascendancy over mankind as that of the ancient Gauls and Britons.'[27]

But perhaps the most important thing for us to note in the eighteenth century is the publication of Cowper's *Ode* in 1780. 'When the British warrior queen . . .' Its affinity with Gray's poem *The Bard*, published in 1754, is clear, Cowper's Druid corresponding to the Welsh Bard of the earlier poem. But the theme develops in a quite different way. Where the Bard pronounces the curse on Edward I and foretells the extinction of his line, the Druid does not merely prophesy the downfall of Rome, but the future glory of Boudicca's posterity and the great empire that shall be theirs.

> 'Regions Caesar never knew
> Thy posterity shall sway,
> Where his eagles never flew,
> None invincible as they.'

And that, of course, is the nub of the matter. Stricken deer he might be in private life, but in politics Cowper was a sturdy patriot; liberal to the cause of African negroes, he had no sympathy with the rebellious colonists in America. And the *Ode*, written during the War of American Independence, expresses his hopes for the triumph of British arms in that struggle, undeterred by any reflection that 'Boadicea' might be less incongruous in the camp of Washington. The prophecy was to be a failure, the poem a triumph. It has found its way into most anthologies and is 'known to every schoolboy'; together with the statue on the Thames Embankment, it has fixed the image of 'Boadicea' in the tradition of our times.

Though a favourite of its author, Tennyson's poem on *Boadicea* has never been as popular as that of Cowper. There is no suggestion that it was connected with the eighteen-hundredth anniversary of the rebellion, although it was written in 1860, when he was already Laureate. He describes it as 'an experiment': the experiment being a metrical one, for it is an attempt to reproduce in English the galliambic metre of Catullus's famous poem *Atys*. There is an interesting reference to it in the *Memoirs*.[28] 'A few weeks later he read aloud to Emily a fiercely brilliant poem, which he had just composed, on the subject of Boadicea—an echo, as he called it, of a very unusual and extremely difficult Latin metre of Catullus. He was very pleased with the success of this poem and torn between the desire to get his friends' opinions of it and the fear that it might become known and imitated before publication. One cold windy day when the Duke of Argyll was at Farringford he took him into the middle of a large stubble field under the downs and there recited the poem to him from beginning to end under the strictest pledge of secrecy.' The pledge was hardly necessary: the poem has found no imitators, and probably few readers. The trouble is in the metre. It was a good idea that the metre in which Catullus had described the frenzies of the devotees of an orgiastic religion might serve for the frantic prophesies of the British Queen. But English is not Latin, and Tennyson's own formula 'if only people would read it straight like prose just as it is written, it would come all right', does not seem to work. Its author, at least, could read it with the proper force and cadence. It remained a favourite of his to the end of his life, and when in 1890 he made readings of his own poetry for the gramophone an extract from *Boadicea* was included. We may indeed agree that, like the *Atys* itself, it is a fiercely brilliant poem. Nor will the Latinist fail to note the curious parallel, in the theme of the Island and the Ocean, between Tennyson's poem and the splendid but anonymous lines written by a contemporary in honour of the Claudian conquest.[29] Compare

'Semota et vasto disiuncta Britannia ponto
cinctaque inaccessis horrida litoribus,
quam pater invictis Nereus velaverat undis
quam fallax aestu circuit Oceanus . . .'

with Tennyson's lines . . .

'Fear not, isle of blowing woodland, isle of silvery parapets,
Tho' the Roman eagle shadow thee, tho' the gathering enemy narrow thee,
Thou shalt wax and he shall dwindle, then shalt be the mighty one yet!
Thine the victory, thine the glory, thine the deeds to be celebrated.
Thine the myriad-rolling oceans, light and shadow illimitable,

Thine the lands of lasting summer, many-blossoming Paradises,
Thine the North and thine the South and thine the
   battle-thunder of God.'

At about the same time the sculptor Thomas Thornycroft
first conceived the idea of a major work on the Boadicea theme.
The gestation was to be a long one: and its creator died years
before it was placed on its present site on the Thames Embankment.[30] Thornycroft took seriously the obligations of a member
of the Royal Academy to work on subjects drawn from English
history, and had already produced statues of Alfred the Great
and Charles I, besides official commissions dealing with the
Royal family. These had brought him into contact with
Prince Albert, who first suggested to him the subject of
Boadicea. In the Royal Academy Exhibition of 1864 he
showed a 'Colossal Head of Boadicea, part of a chariot group
now in progress'. The Prince Consort took a great interest in
the project, lending white horses from the Royal Mews as
models, and offering to find a suitable site in London—the
central arch of Hyde Park entrance was put forward at one
stage. But the group was a colossal one, and Thornycroft had
other interests in the field of engineering. Prince Albert died
before it was finished: there was talk of a Government commission in 1871, but it came to nothing. The plaster cast was
completed at last, and stood for years in a studio in Thornycroft's house in Wilton Place. He died in 1885: a few years later
the London County Council started to excavate the tumulus
in Parliament Hill Fields 'traditionally' known as Boadicea's
grave. At this point the sculptor's son, John Thornycroft,
offered to present the chariot group to the public, and to contri-
bute towards the cost of casting it. The tumulus was in mind
as a site, but the Society of Antiquaries poured cold water on
any connexion with Boadicea. Then Sir William Bull, the
member of the L.C.C. for the district, took in hand the problem
of a suitable site. The Temple Arch was considered and dismissed: the final—and admirable—choice being the Embankment. Cast in bronze, partly paid for by public subscription,
and on a pedestal provided by the L.C.C., the group was
erected in 1902—almost half a century after work on it had
first begun.

Inevitably, Cowper's poem was drawn on for the inscription 'Regions Caesar never knew . . .' None could have been better fitted to the temper of the times. For this was the high noon of the imperial idea in Britain. The Empire seemed to have found a new unity in the Boer War, and its successful conclusion promised to lead to a more glorious future. It was not unnatural that comparisons should be made between the British and the Roman Empire: the more so, as so many of the young men who went out from the universities to govern it had received a classical education. The comparison was often drawn in the scholarship of the period: as, for example, in B. W. Henderson's *Life and Principate of the Emperor Nero*, published in 1903. The Indian Mutiny is present in Henderson's mind as he tells the story of the Boudicca rebellion—'We English, too, have had to face the doom in India, which fell out of a sunny heaven on amazed Camulodunum, and we too may know how the Romans died. They waited the oncoming fury with the courage, not only of despair, but of grim Roman ferocity and courage.' His sympathy thus engaged with the imperial forces, Henderson had little for the cause of the native. Besides, the Britons, though *in* this island, were not really of it; they had the misfortune not to be English. 'It were notwithstanding but maudlin sentiment to bewail the Roman victory. The revenge was one of other greater races than the Briton . . . The Roman conquest was Britain's first step along the path to her wider Empire.'[31]

Few, now, would write like this. If the British Empire has had a wider sway, the Roman would appear to better advantage on the score of durability. But the statue on the Embankment still stands for something. For the general educated public it enters into the received idea of Roman Britain; at the very least, it has indelibly impressed the idea of the scythed chariot, to the despair of the archaeologist (see p. 19). Boudicca and Caratacus are the two figures who really stand out, for the layman, from the period of Roman Britain; they do not play the same part as Vercingetorix in France or Arminius in Germany, but they are there. And this is odd, for the representative figures might have been Cassivellaunus, or Calgacus, who successfully defied Rome. Is this another instance of the peculiarly British fondness for the gallant failure? Or is it, as seems more likely, the combined work of Cowper and Thorny-croft?

We may fitly end this sketch with an author whose dramatic instinct can vie with that of Tacitus himself, and who claims to be 'not without some experience of historical and violent events in our own time'. The first volume of Sir Winston Churchill's *History of the English-Speaking Peoples* contains a fine passage[32] on the rebellion of Boadicea ('relished by the learned as Boudicca'). Of its butcheries he says 'this is probably the most horrible episode which our Island has known. We see the crude and corrupt beginning of a higher civilization blotted out by the ferocious uprising of the native tribes. Still, it is the primary right of men to die and kill for the land they live in, and to punish with exceptional severity all members of their own race who have warmed their hands at the invader's hearth.' The monument on the Thames Embankment 'reminds us of the harsh cry of "Liberty or death" which has echoed down the ages'.

Slight as it is, this outline will have shown how the historical reputation of Boudicca has, over the past five centuries, served several turns. It has been made use of for propaganda for the monarchy of Elizabeth I, for anti-feminism, for imperialism, alike that of the eighteenth century and of its late Victorian heyday, and for the simpler patriotism that identifies itself with all who defend this island against its invaders. There is no reason to suppose that these metamorphoses are at an end. Boudicca may yet have a part to play as the unenlightened opponent of a European Common Market. She may again provide a theme for imaginative literature; in Fletcher, Cowper, and Tennyson it has not lacked distinguished authors, though it has found none of them at his best. But, looking ahead from the nineteenth-hundredth anniversary, it is surely from archaeology that we should expect new light to be thrown on the great rebellion. The characteristic achievement of our age is to find the slave chains of the Druids, in place of speculating on their views about the immortality of the soul. Before many years have passed we may confidently expect to know a good deal more about the settlement and society of the Iceni and their neighbours. The investigation of sites belonging to the early phases of Roman penetration into Icenian territory may well elucidate the aftermath of the rebellion; new evidence for its course may be forthcoming from London, St. Albans, Colchester, and elsewhere. By the two-thousandth anniversary, or more probably long before it, such a collection of evidence as we have assembled will have an archaic air. It is right, however, to recognize the limitations as well as the possibilities of archaeology. The rebellion of Boudicca has an established place in British history and tradition. Almost nothing of it would be known had not Cornelius Tacitus referred to it in the *Life* of Agricola, and had he not, in the *Annals*, seen fit to turn aside from the recital of the crimes and follies of Nero's earlier years to give a brief but highly-wrought account of disaster in Britain.

APPENDIX I

The Tacitean Narrative

I. *Agricola*, 14, 4–16, 2

Suetonius hinc Paulinus biennio prosperas res habuit, subactis nationibus firmatisque praesidiis; quorum fiducia Monam insulam ut vires rebellibus ministrantem adgressus terga occasioni patefecit.

Namque absentia legati remoto metu Britanni agitare inter se mala servitutis, conferre iniurias et interpretando accendere: nihil profici patientia nisi ut graviora tamquam ex facili tolerantibus imperentur. singulos sibi olim reges fuisse, nunc binos imponi, e quibus legatus in sanguinem, procurator in bona saeviret. aeque discordiam praepositorum, aeque concordiam subiectis exitiosam. alterius manum centuriones, alterius servos vim et contumelias miscere. nihil iam cupiditati, nihil libidini exceptum. in proelio fortiorem esse qui spoliet: nunc ab ignavis plerumque et inbellibus eripi domos, abstrahi liberos, iniungi dilectus, tamquam mori tantum pro patria nescientibus. quantulum enim transisse militum, si sese Britanni numerent? sic Germanias excussisse iugum: et flumine, non Oceano defendi. sibi patriam coniuges parentes, illis avaritiam et luxuriam causas belli esse. recessuros, ut divus Iulius recessisset, modo virtutem maiorum suorum aemularentur. neve proelii unius aut alterius eventu pavescerent: plus impetus, maiorem constantiam penes miseros esse. iam Britannorum etiam deos misereri, qui Romanum ducem absentem, qui relegatum in alia insula exercitum detinerent; iam ipsos, quod difficillimum fuerit, deliberare. porro in eius modi consiliis periculosius esse deprehendi quam audere.

His atque talibus in vicem instincti, Boudicca generis regii femina duce (neque enim sexum in imperiis discernunt) sumpsere universi bellum; ac sparsos per castella milites consectati, expugnatis praesidiis ipsam coloniam invasere ut sedem servitutis, nec ullum in barbaris saevitiae genus omisit ira et victoria. quod nisi Paulinus cognito provinciae motu propere subvenisset, amissa Britannia foret; quam unius proelii fortuna veteri patientiae restituit, tenentibus arma plerisque, quos conscientia defectionis et propius ex legato timor agitabat, ne quamquam egregius cetera adroganter in deditos et ut suae cuiusque iniuriae ultor durius consuleret.

II. *Annals, XIV*, 29–39

Caesennio Paeto et Petronio Turpiliano consulibus gravis clades in Britannia accepta; in qua neque A. Didius legatus, ut memoravi, nisi parta retinuerat, et successor Veranius modicis excursibus Siluras populatus, quin ultra bellum proferret, morte prohibitus est, magna, dum vixit, severitatis fama, supremis testamenti verbis ambitionis manifestus: quippe multa in Neronem adulatione addidit subiecturum ei provinciam fuisse, si biennio proximo vixisset. sed tum Paulinus Suetonius obtinebat Britannos, scientia militiae et rumore populi qui neminem sine aemulo sinit, Corbulonis concertator, receptaeque Armeniae decus aequare domitis perduellibus cupiens. igitur Monam insulam, incolis validam et receptaculum perfugarum, adgredi parat, navisque fabricatur plano alveo adversus breve et incertum. sic pedes; equites vado secuti aut altiores inter undas adnantes equis tramisere.

Stabat pro litore diversa acies, densa armis virisque, intercursantibus feminis; in modum Furiarum veste ferali, crinibus deiectis faces praeferebant; Druidaeque circum, preces, diras sublatis ad caelum manibus fundentes, novitate aspectus perculere militem ut quasi haerentibus membris immobile corpus vulneribus praeberent. dein cohortationibus ducis et se ipsi stimulantes ne muliebre et fanaticum agmen pavescerent, inferunt signa sternuntque obvios et igni suo involvunt. praesidium posthac impositum victis excisique luci saevis superstitionibus sacri: nam cruore captivo adolere aras et hominum fibris consulere deos fas habebant. haec agenti Suetonio repentina defectio provinciae nuntiatur.

Rex Icenorum Prasutagus, longa opulentia clarus, Caesarem heredem duasque filias scripserat, tali obsequio ratus regnumque et domum suam procul iniuria fore. quod contra vertit, adeo ut regnum per centuriones, domus per servos velut capta vastarentur. iam primum uxor eius Boudicca verberibus adfecta et filiae stupro violatae sunt: praecipui quique Icenorum, quasi cunctam regionem muneri accepissent, avitis bonis exuuntur, et propinqui regis inter mancipia habebantur. qua contumelia et metu graviorum, quando in formam provinciae cesserant, rapiunt arma, commotis ad rebellationem Trinobantibus et qui alii nondum servitio fracti resumere libertatem occultis coniurationibus pepigerant, acerrimo in veteranos odio. quippe in coloniam Camulodunum recens deducti pellebant domibus, exturbabant agris, captivos, servos appellando, foventibus impotentiam veteranorum militibus similitudine vitae et spe eiusdem licentiae. ad hoc templum divo Claudio constitutum quasi arx aeternae dominationis aspiciebatur, delectique sacerdotes specie religionis omnis fortunas effundebant. nec arduum videbatur excindere coloniam nullis munimentis saeptam; quod ducibus nostris parum provisum erat, dum amoenitati prius quam usui consulitur.

Inter quae nulla palam causa delapsum Camuloduni simulacrum Victoriae ac retro conversu quasi cederet hostibus. et feminae in furorem turbatae adesse exitium canebant, externosque fremitus in curia eorum auditos; consonuisse ululatibus theatrum visamque speciem in aestuario Tamesae subversae coloniae: iam Oceanus cruento aspectu, dilabente aestu humanorum corporum effigies relictae, ut Britannis ad spem, ita veteranis ad metum trahebantur. sed quia procul Suetonius aberat, petivere a Cato Deciano procuratore auxilium. ille haud amplius quam ducentos sine iustis armis misit; et inerat modica militum manus. tutela templi freti et impedientibus qui occulti rebellionis conscii consilia turbabant, neque fossam aut vallum praeduxerunt, neque motis senibus et feminis iuventus sola restitit: quasi media pace incauti multitudine barbarorum circumveniuntur. et cetera quidem impetu direpta aut incensa sunt: templum in quo se miles conglobaverat biduo obsessum expugnatumque. et victor Britannus Petilio Ceriali, legato legionis nonae, in subsidium adventanti obvius fudit legionem et quod peditum interfecit: Cerialis cum equitibus evasit in castra et munimentis defensus est. qua clade et odiis provinciae quam avaritia eius in bellum egerat trepidus procurator Catus in Galliam transiit.

At Suetonius mira constantia medios inter hostis Londinium perrexit, cognomento quidem coloniae non insigne, sed copia negotiatorum et commeatuum maxime celebre. ibi ambiguus an illam sedem bello deligeret, circumspecta infrequentia militis, satisque magnis documentis temeritatem Petilii coercitam, unius oppidi damno servare universa statuit. neque fletu et lacrimis auxilium eius orantium flexus est quin daret profectionis signum et comitantis in partem agminis acciperet: si quos imbellis sexus aut fessa aetas vel loci dulcedo attinuerat ab hoste oppressi sunt. eadem clades municipio Verulamio fuit, quia barbari omissis castellis praesidiisque militarium, quod uberrimum spolianti et defendentibus intutum, laeti praeda et laborum segnes petebant. ad septuaginta milia civium et sociorum iis quae memoravi locis cecidisse constitit.

neque enim capere aut venundare aliudve quod belli commercium, sed caedes patibula ignes cruces, tamquam reddituri supplicium at praerepta interim ultione, festinabant.

Iam Suetonio quarta decima legio cum vexillariis vicesimanis et e proximis auxiliares, decem ferme milia armatorum erant, cum omittere cunctationem et congredi acie parat. deligitque locum artis faucibus et a tergo silva clausum, satis cognito nihil hostium nisi in fronte et apertam planitiem esse sine metu insidiarum. igitur legionarius frequens ordinibus, levis circum armatura, conglobatus pro cornibus eques adstitit. at Britannorum copiae passim per catervas et turmas exultabant, quanta non alias multitudo, et animo adeo feroci ut coniuges quoque testis victoriae secum traherent plaustrisque imponerent quae super extremum ambitum campi posuerant.

Boudicca curru filias prae se vehens, ut quamque nationem accesserat, solitum quidem Britannis feminarum ductu bellare testabatur, sed tunc non ut tantis maioribus ortam regnum et opes, verum ut unam e vulgo libertatem amissam, confectum verberibus corpus, contrectatam filiarum pudicitiam ulcisci. eo provectas Romanorum cupidines ut non corpora, ne senectam quidem aut virginitatem impollutam relinquant. adesse tamen deos iustae vindictae: cecidisse legionem quae proelium ausa sit; ceteros castris occultari aut fugam circumspicere. ne strepitum quidem et clamorem tot milium, nedum impetus et manus perlaturos: si copias armatorum, si causas belli secum expenderent, vincendum illa acie vel cadendum esse. id mulieri destinatum: viverent viri et servirent.

Ne Suetonius quidem in tanto discrimine silebat: quamquam confideret virtuti, tamen exhortationes et preces miscebat ut spernerent sonores barbarorum et inanis minas: plus illic feminarum quam iuventutis aspici. imbellis, inermis cessuros statim ubi ferrum virtutemque vincentium toties fusi adgnovissent. etiam in multis legionibus paucos qui proelia profligarent; gloriaeque eorum accessurum quod modica manus universi exercitus famam adipiscerentur. conferti tantum et pilis emissis post umbonibus et gladiis stragem caedemque continuarent, praedae immemores: parta victoria cuncta ipsis cessura. is ardor verba ducis sequebatur, ita se ad intorquenda pila expedierat vetus miles et multa proeliorum experientia ut certus eventus Suetonius daret pugnae signum.

Ac primum legio gradu immota et angustias loci pro munimento retinens, postquam in propius suggressos hostis certo iactu tela exhauserat, velut cuneo erupit. idem auxiliarium impetus; et eques protentis hastis perfringit quod obvium et validum erat. ceteri terga praebuere, difficili effugio, quia circumiecta vehicula saepserant abitus. et miles ne mulierum quidem neci temperabat, confixaque telis etiam iumenta corporum cumulum auxerant. clara et antiquis victoriis par ea die laus parta: quippe sunt qui paulo minus quam octoginta milia Britannorum cecidisse tradant, militum quadringentis ferme interfectis nec multo amplius vulneratis. Boudicca vitam vereno finivit. et Poenius Postumus, praefectus castrorum secundae legionis, cognitis quartadecimanorum vicesimanorumque prosperis rebus, quia pari gloria legionem suam fraudaverat abnueratque contra ritum militiae iussa ducis, se ipse gladio transegit.

Contractus deinde omnis exercitus sub pellibus habitus est ad reliqua belli perpetranda. auxitque copias Caesar missis ex Germania duobus legionariorum milibus, octo auxiliarium cohortibus ac mille equitibus; quorum adventu nonani legionario milite suppleti sunt, cohortes alaeque novis hibernaculis locatae quodque nationum ambiguum aut adversum fuerat igni atque ferro vastatum. sed nihil aeque quam fames adfligebat serendis frugibus incuriosos, et omni aetate ad bellum versa, dum nostros commeatus sibi destinant. gentesque praeferoces tardius ad pacem inclinabant, quia Iulius Classicianus, successor Cato missus et Suetonio discors, bonum publicum privatis simultatibus impediebat disperseratque novum legatum opperiendum esse, sine hostili ira et superbia victoris clementer deditis consulturum. simul in urbem mandabat, nullum proeliorum finem expectarent, nisi succederetur Suetonio, cuius adversa pravitati ipsius, prospera ad fortunam referebat.

Igitur ad spectandum Britanniae statum missus est e libertis Polyclitus, magna Neronis spe posse auctoritate eius non modo inter legatum procuratoremque concordiam gigni, sed et rebellis barbarum animos pace componi. nec defuit Polyclitus quo minus ingenti agmine Italiae Galliaeque gravis, postquam Oceanum transmiserat, militibus quoque nostris terribilis incederet. sed hostibus inrisui fuit apud quos flagrante etiam tum libertate nondum cognita libertinorum potentia erat; mirabanturque quod dux et exercitus tanti belli confector servitiis oboedirent. cuncta tamen ad imperatorem in mollius relata; detentusque rebus gerundis Suetonius, quod postea paucas navis in litore remigiumque in iis amiserat, tamquam durante bello tradere exercitum Petronio Turpiliano qui iam consulatu abierat iubetur. is non inritato hoste neque lacessitus honestum pacis nomen segni otio imposuit.

Translation I. *Agricola*, 14, 4–16, 2

After this Suetonius Paulinus enjoyed two years of success. Tribes were subdued, garrisons strengthened: relying on these measures he attacked the island of Mona, as a source of strength to the rebels, but by so doing exposed himself to attack from the rear.

With the governor away, the fears of the Britons had been removed, and they began to discuss among themselves the evils of slavery, to compare their grievances, and to incite each other by the construction they placed upon them. Nothing, they argued, would be gained by patience—unless it were the imposition of still harsher burdens, on the grounds that their tolerance was all too ready. Once they had one king for each tribe, now two had been set over them, and of these the governor exercised a tyranny over their persons and the procurator over their property. Whether their overlords were at odds with each other, or in agreement, it was equally disastrous for the subjugated: centurions were the tools of the one, slaves of the other, and they heaped injury on insult. Nothing now was exempt from greed and lust. In battle, the spoils went to the stronger: but now it was generally by unwarlike cowards that their homes were torn away from them, their children dragged off, and conscription imposed on themselves—as though it were only for their own country that Britons did not know how to die. And, after all, what a contemptible little army the Romans had brought over, if the Britons counted their own numbers! That was how the Germans had shaken off the Roman yoke, and they were protected by a river, not by the Ocean itself. The Britons would be fighting for their country, their wives, and their parents, the Romans for greed and luxury. They would retreat—as the late Emperor Julius had retreated—if only the Britons would find again their ancestors' valour. Nor should they be dismayed by the outcome of a single battle, nor yet a second: the prosperous might have more *élan*, but the oppressed had more resolution. Even the gods were now taking pity on the Britons, for they were detaining the governor, banished as it were, in another island. They themselves were now consulting together—and that had always been the hardest thing to achieve— moreover, in pursuing policies of this kind, it was more dangerous to be detected than to be bold.

Inflamed by these, or similar, arguments, and under the leadership of Boudicca, a woman of the Royal house (for they do not discriminate against women in the matter of military command)— they took up arms in a general rising. They pursued the troops who were dispersed among the smaller forts, overwhelmed the camps, and then stormed the colony itself, as the very seat of slavery. Their barbarous anger in the hour of victory shrank from no form of atrocity. Had not Suetonius come to the rescue when he heard of the general rising of the province, Britain would have been lost. As it was, the issue of a single battle restored it to its old obedience. Even so, many of the rebels remained under arms, only too conscious of their own disloyalty, and very naturally apprehensive about the governor, fearing that—however admirable in other respects—he might act harshly to those who gave themselves up and pursue a cruel policy, for he was a man who avenged every wrong done to him.

Translation II. *Annals, XIV*, 29–39

In the consulship of Caesennius Paetus and Petronius Turpilianus a terrible disaster was suffered in Britain. I have already narrated how, in that province, the governor A. Didius did no more than maintain the *status quo*: his successor Veranius made a number of raids against the Silures, but died before he could extend the war further. In his life his reputation was one of great independence, but the last words of his will convicted him of self-seeking, for after gross flattery of Nero he added that he would have presented him with the whole province, subjugated, had he lived two years longer. But by now Suetonius Paulinus was in charge of Britain. He was Corbulo's rival in military skill, as in popular gossip, which leaves no one without a rival, and he was eager to achieve military victories to match the glory of the reconquest of Armenia. He therefore planned an expedition against the island of Mona, which was itself thickly populated, and had offered sanctuary to many who fled from Roman power. Flat-bottomed boats were built to cope with the shifting shallows; these transported the infantry; the cavalry got across by finding the fords, or, in deeper waters, swimming beside their horses.

The shore was lined by a motley battle array. There were warriors with their arms, and women rushing to and fro among their ranks, dressed in black, like furies, their hair dishevelled, brandishing torches, and Druids with their arms raised to heaven and calling down terrible curses. The soldiers, paralysed by this strange spectacle, stood still and offered themselves as a target for wounds. But at last the promptings of the general—and their own rallying of each other—urged them not to be frightened of a mob of women and fanatics. They advanced the standards, cut down all who met them, and swallowed them up in their own fires. After this, a garrison was placed over the conquered islanders, and the groves sacred to savage rites were cut down—for their religion enjoined them to drench their altars with the blood of prisoners, and to find out the will of the gods by consulting the entrails of human beings. While Suetonius was thus engaged, he was informed of a sudden rising in the province.

Prasutagus, King of the Iceni, distinguished by the prosperity he had long enjoyed, had died, and left the Emperor as heir, together with his two daughters. His hope had been that with such subservience the kingdom, and his own property, would remain inviolate, but it fell out far otherwise. Both were plundered as though they were the spoils of war, the kingdom by centurions, the Royal household by the procurator's slaves. The first outrage was the flogging of his wife Boudicca and the rape of his daughters: then the Icenian nobles were deprived of their ancestral estates as though the Romans had been presented with the whole country, and the King's relatives were treated as though they were household slaves. These outrages, and the fear of worse, now that they had been reduced to the status of a province, moved the Iceni to arms. They were joined by the Trinobantes, and other tribes who were unsubdued by slavery, and who had secretly conspired together to regain their freedom. The veterans were the especial object of their hatred. These men, recently settled at Camulodunum, had been turning them out of their homes, taking away their lands, and calling them prisoners and slaves. The soldiers did nothing to check the insolence of the veterans, for they were men of the same stamp and hoped for similar licence when their own time came. To add to this, the Temple of Claudius seemed to have been established as the very citadel of enduring slavery, and its chosen priests, under the guise of a religious cult, were squandering the wealth of the whole country. To attack a position undefended by fortifications seemed no arduous undertaking; indeed, the Roman governors had scandalously neglected to take precautions, putting amenities before the needs of defence.

At this point, and for no apparent cause, the statue of Victory at Camulodunum fell down, its back turned as though yielding to an enemy. Frenzied women prophesied destruction: saying that barbarian yells had been heard in the senate house, the theatre had echoed with the howlings of wild beasts, and a vision of a phantom colony had been seen in the Thames estuary, sacked and destroyed: nay, the very ocean reeked of blood, and the ebbing tide had left the imprint of corpses on the shore. All this induced hope in the Britons, and fear in the veterans. But the governor was away, and they sent for help to the procurator, Catus Decianus. He sent them hardly two hundred men, without proper equipment; there was a small garrison on the spot: and they relied on the temple as a strongpoint. Misled by a fifth column, who threw their plans into confusion, they took no steps to construct a rampart or ditch, nor to evacuate old people and defend the place with men of military age. Devoid of precautions as though in time of peace, they let themselves be surrounded by huge numbers of barbarians. Everything else was overrun in the attack, or went up in flames, but the soldiers concentrated in the temple and held out for two days. Then it was overwhelmed. The victorious Britons routed Petilius Cerealis, the commander of the Ninth Legion, as he was marching to the rescue. His infantry was cut to pieces: he himself escaped to the legionary camp with his cavalry and took shelter behind its walls. The procurator Catus Decianus, whose greed had driven the province into war, was so horrified by this disaster and by the hatred against him that he fled to Gaul.

But Suetonius, with remarkable steadfastness, pressed on through the midst of the enemy to Londinium, a place not dignified by the name of a colony, but crowded with merchants and provisions. He was uncertain whether to make it a military centre, but after discovering its lack of troops, and well aware of the price paid by Cerialis for his rashness, he decided to save the whole situation by the sacrifice of this single town. No tears, no laments from those who begged his help could prevent him from giving the signal for departure. Those who could keep up with him were given a place in the column: but all who, because of their sex or age, or love for the place, chose to stay, were butchered by the enemy. The same fate overtook the *municipium* of Verulamium. For the barbarians paid no attention to forts or garrisons, but made for the richest booty under the feeblest protection, for they loved plunder and shrank from toils. It has been established that some 70,000 persons, Roman citizens and allies, were massacred in the three places I have mentioned. The Britons had no thought of taking prisoners or selling them as slaves, nor for any of the usual commerce of war; but only of slaughter, the gibbet, fire, and the cross. They knew they would have to pay the penalty: meantime they hurried on to exact, as it were, vengeance in advance.

By now Suetonius had with him the Fourteenth Legion, and a detachment of the Twentieth, together with auxiliary troops from the nearest fort, a total of some 10,000 men, and he decided to make an end of delay and to seek engagement in battle. He chose a position in a narrow defile, protected from behind by a forest. Here he could be sure that there would be no enemy except in front, where an open plain gave no cover for ambushes. He therefore drew up the legionaries in close order, with the light-armed auxiliaries on either flank, and massed the cavalry on the wings. The British forces, on the other hand, ranged over a wide area in bands of infantry and cavalry. Never had they massed in such great numbers, and they were so confident of victory that they had brought their wives and children with them to witness it, and placed them on wagons at the edge of the battlefield.

Boudicca drove round in a chariot, her daughters with her. As they reached each tribal contingent, she proclaimed that the Britons were well used to the leadership of women in battle. But she did not come among them now as a descendant of mighty ancestors, eager to avenge her lost wealth and kingdom. Rather was she an ordinary woman, fighting for her lost freedom, her bruised body, and the outraged virginity of her daughters. Roman greed no longer spared their bodies, old people were killed, virgins raped. But the gods would grant a just vengeance: the legion which had dared to fight had perished: the others were skulking in their camps and looking for means of escape. They would never face the roar and din of the British thousands, much less their charges and their grappling hand-to-hand. Let them consider how many they had under arms, and why! Then they would know that on that day it was victory or death. That was her resolve, as a woman, the men could live, if they liked, and be slaves.

Suetonius, too, did not keep silent at this moment of crisis. Confident as he was of his men's courage, he thought it best to add encouragement and appeals. 'Don't pay any attention to the noises of these savages,' he said, 'nor to their empty threats: there are more women than soldiers in their ranks. They are unwarlike and ill armed: when they see the weapons and valour of troops who have beaten them so often they're going to crack. Even in a force with many legions, few win battle honours—what glory awaits you, a small band that is going to win the renown of a whole army! Keep together: throw your javelins: strike with the points of your shields: and carry on from there. Don't give a thought to booty: win the victory, and you've got the lot.' His words were received with enthusiasm: the battle-hardened soldiers were itching to throw their javelins: Suetonius knew he could count on victory and gave the signal for battle.

At first the legion stood its ground, using the defile for protection. When the enemy approached more closely up the slope, they discharged their javelins with unerring aim. Then they burst forward in wedge formation, as did the auxiliary forces, and the cavalry, lances at the ready, broke down all serious resistance. The rest of the Britons turned to flight, but this the ring of wagons made impossible. The Romans did not spare the women, and the bodies of baggage-animals, pierced with spears, were added to the piles of corpses. It was a glorious victory, equal to those of the good old days: some estimate as many as 80,000 British dead: there were only

400 Romans killed, and scarcely more wounded. Boudicca ended her life with poison. As for Poenius Postumus, camp commandant of the Second Legion, he fell on his sword when he heard of the honours won by the Fourteenth and the Twentieth—for he had cheated his own men of a like distinction and disobeyed his commander's orders, in defiance of army regulations.

Then the whole army was concentrated and kept under canvas to finish the war. The Emperor increased their strength by sending as reinforcements from Germany two thousand legionary soldiers, eight auxiliary infantry battalions, and a thousand cavalry. These were enough to bring the Ninth Legion up to strength: the infantry and cavalry were stationed in new winter quarters: the territory of all tribes that had been hostile or neutral was laid waste with fire and sword. But famine was the worst of their hardships: they had omitted to sow the crops and brought every man into the army, regardless of age, expecting that they could secure our supplies for themselves. The British tribes were obstinate and little inclined for peace—especially as the procurator, Julius Classicianus, who had replaced Catus and did not get on with Suetonius, allowed his private dislikes to interfere with the public interest. Indeed, he kept urging them to wait for a new governor who would be lenient to the conquered, without the bitterness of an enemy and the arrogance of the victor. He reported to Rome that there would be no end to campaigning unless Suetonius was superseded; and he attributed his failures to his base qualities, his victories to luck.

So Polyclitus, one of the imperial freedmen, was sent out to investigate affairs in Britain. It was Nero's hope that his authority would be sufficient to reconcile the governor and the procurator, and to pacify the warlike and rebellious Britons. Polyclitus played his part, burdened Italy and Gaul with a huge retinue, and after crossing the Ocean, struck terror even into a Roman army. The barbarians only thought him ridiculous: liberty still prevailed with them: and they could not understand how an army and a general who could complete so great a war should obey the commands of slaves. However, everything was toned down in the report to the Emperor. Suetonius's term of office was prolonged, but when, shortly afterwards, he lost a few ships and their crews on the shore, he was superseded as though protracting the war by Petronius Turpilianus, who had just laid down his consulship. The latter neither provoked the enemy nor suffered loss at their hands, conferring the honourable name of peace on what was really scandalous inertia.

APPENDIX II

The Name Boudicca

'Boudicca' has by now generally superseded the Victorian 'Boadicea', and is the form which will be used in this book. It does not, however, satisfy the Celtic philologists. Professor K. H. Jackson has kindly sent the following note on the name and its pronunciation:

'Boudicca.' This is the form written by Tacitus, apparently, but it is wrong; it should have only one *C*. I should very much like to see 'Boudica' adopted; everyone has been so pleased with the emendation of the old 'Boadicea', believing it to be confirmed by Welsh, but they have not got it perfectly right. The name is a derivative of * bouda, 'victory', and is of course the Mod. Welsh *buddug*, 'Victoria'. But *buddug* is a secondary development, with vowel-harmony from (older) *buddig*, and this is from British 'Boudīcā', which is the correct form of the lady's name. 'Bouddiccā' would give Buddech; 'Boudiccā' would give Buddoch; and Boudica would give *Buddeg*. The only possible solution is 'Boudīcā', from * bouda and the—ico—adjectival termination.

On the name 'Iceni' he adds: 'No comment: seems obscure. Ixworth and Ickenham are pretty certainly not connected: see Ekwall's Oxford Dictionary on these names . . . Ekwall *does* think the river-name Itchen comes from Iceni, and he may be right'.

APPENDIX III

The Date of the Rebellion

A.D. 60 was first put forward as the date of the Rebellion by J. Asbach, *Analecta historica et epigraphica* (Bonn, 1878), 8 ff. It was adopted by B. W. Henderson, *The Life and Principate of the Emperor Nero* (1903), 20b: 477 f., and has now been reinforced by the powerful authority of Sir Ronald Syme, *Tacitus* (Oxford, 1958), vol. ii, 765. The gist of Syme's argument is that the total of events, from the outbreak of the rebellion to the supersession of Suetonius Paulinus, is too much to fit into a single year. Hence 'it is clear that Tacitus has been guilty of an inadvertence in dating. The revolt must have begun in 60.'

The question will bear further inquiry. For Tacitus is quite explicit . . . 'Caesennio Paeto et Petronio Turpiliano consulibus (i.e. 61) gravis clades in Britannia accepta . . .' Agreed that the total of events will overlap into a second year, why should Petronius Turpilianus not have arrived in Britain in the early part of 62? Certainly his colleague Caesennius Paetus, who was sent out to the east after his consulship, reached Cappadocia in 62. Against this it must be said (i) an inscription (CIL vi. i. 597), mentions Paetus and a certain P. Calvisius Ruso as consuls on March 1. This suggests that Petronius Turpilianus was replaced by a *consul suffectus* (a common enough practice at this period), and sent out to Britain for the emergency of 61. However, the inscription cannot be taken as conclusive, for it is sometimes regarded as of Flavian date, as pointed out by Henderson. But, further, (ii) Tacitus's phrase about Petronius on his arrival in Britain 'he had just laid down his consulship' (*qui iam a consulatu abierat*) gains much more point if it refers to a man who had only a tenure of three months, than if used of one who had completed a full year. (Indeed, it would then be an indirect way of saying—'I forgot to mention, by then it was the next year'!) (iii) There is also the consideration that three years

144

was, at this time, the normal tenure for governors of Britain. This was the expectation of Veranius, who took over in 57, but died within a year. Suetonius, taking over in 58, would presumably have been recalled late in 60 but for the Rebellion. As for Petronius, he is known to have been *curator aquarum* in Rome in 64; if he came to Britain in 61 that would give him a three-year tenure. (iv) On this reasoning, we can better understand Tacitus's phrase that, after the inquiry of Polyclitus, '*detentusque rebus gerundis Suetonius*', i.e. he was retained, not only as a result of the inquiry, but also as an extension of his tenure of office. (v) Finally, it can be shown that Tacitus also telescopes his dates in the Armenian campaigns. All this adds up, in our view, to a strong presumption in favour of 60, and we have therefore adopted that year as the date of the outbreak of the Rebellion. But it is only right to say that we do not think it completely disposes of 61.

APPENDIX IV

The Tombstone of Classicianus

Parts of the tombstone were found at two different times. With other similar large stone blocks they had been used for the foundations of a bastion added to the Roman city wall, probably in the middle of the fourth century (*Arch. J.*, cxii (1955) pp. 20–42). The first of these discoveries was made in 1852 (*Arch. J.*, x (1853) p. 3), the fragment reading DIS[M]ANIBVS . . . F] AB(I) ALPINI CLASSICIANI, and although claimed by Roach Smith as the tombstone of the procurator (*Roman London*, p. 28, Pl 3), the association was thought by R. G. Collingwood to have been improbable (*R.C.M.H. Roman London*, 1927, p. 171). The matter was placed beyond any doubt in 1935 when another fragment was found during the construction of a new sub-station (*Ant. J.*, xvi (1936) pp. 1–7). This gave the last three lines of the inscription, reading: PROC·PROVINC·BRITA[NN]/ IVLIA·INDI·FILIA·PACATA·I[NDIANA(?)] VXOR (for revised reading—*Ant. J.*, xvi (1936) p. 208; *J.R.S.*, xxvi (1936) p. 265). All the fragments have now been placed in their respective positions and the whole imposing monument now has an honoured place in the British Museum (Pl. XI).

NOTES

Abbreviations

CAH = Cambridge Ancient History; CIL = Corpus Inscriptionum Latinarum; PIR = Prosopographia Imperii Romani; PW = Pauly-Wissowa, Reäl Encyclopädie.

Chapter 1

[1] The best general study of the archaeology of East Anglia is R. Rainbird Clarke, *East Anglia*, 1960, which includes a full bibliography. More detailed accounts of sites are to be found in the volumes of *Norfolk Archaeology* and the *Proceedings of the Suffolk Institute of Archaeology*. Other important studies are: R. Rainbird Clarke, 'The Iron Age in Norfolk and Suffolk', *Archaeological Journal*, xcvi (1939), and J. E. Saintly and R. Rainbird Clarke, 'A Century of Norfolk Prehistory', *Norfolk Archaeology*, xxix (1946). The most important collections of material are at Moyse's Hall, Bury St. Edmunds; University Museum of Archaeology and Ethnology, Cambridge; Museum of Natural History, Archaeology and Ethnology, Ipswich, and the Castle Museum, Norwich.

[2] *Prehistoric Society Proceedings*, xix (1953), pp. 1–40.

[3] *Proceedings Prehistoric Society of East Anglia*, vii (1933), pp. 231–262.

[4] Pitt Rivers, *Excavations in Cranborne Chase*, 1887, etc. The greater part of rural life during the Roman period in Britain, although it grew and prospered, especially in the third and fourth centuries, remained unaffected by civilizing influences. This rather suggests that the native population of the countryside was deliberately excluded from the standards of life reflected in the towns and country houses of the landowners, possibly to maintain a cheap source of labour.

[5] Elgee, *Early Man in North-East Yorkshire*, 1930, p. 186.

[6] Writing in 1949, Mr. R. Rainbird Clarke could only list the anthropoid dagger from Hertford Warren, a few brooches and some horse trappings which could belong to the post-conquest period.

[7] *Prehistoric Society Proceedings*, xxi (1955), pp. 198–227.

[8] *Prehistoric Society Proceedings*, xx (1954), pp. 27–86.

[9] *Prehistoric Society Proceedings*, xvii (1951), pp. 214–25.

[10] The torc from Bawsey (*Antiquaries Journal*, xxiv (1944), pp. 149–51);

the terminal of a torc from North Creake (*Archaeological Journal*, cvi (1949), pp. 59–61).

[11] *Verulamium, A Belgic and two Roman Cities*, 1936, 16 (Research Report of the Society of Antiquaries of London).

[12] 'The Belgic Dynasties of Britain and their Coins', *Archaeologia*, xc (1944), pp. 1–48 and 'The Origins of Coinage in Britain: a reappraisal', *Problems of the Iron Age in Southern Britain*, pp. 97–302.

[13] This inscription consists of a list of achievements carefully selected and worded by Augustus himself to hand down to posterity. It was put up in the form of a monument all over the Empire and it so happens that the one at Ancyra is the best preserved.

[14] 'Britain between the Invasions (54 B.C.–A.D. 43): A Study in Ancient Diplomacy', in *Aspects of Archaeology in Britain and Beyond*, 1951, p. 342.

[15] *Bagendon: A Belgic Oppidum*, Elsie M. Clifford, 1961.

[16] *Leicestershire Archaeological Society Trans.*, xxvi (1950), pp. 17–82.

[17] *Excavations at the Jewry Wall Site, Leicester*, 1948, p. 4 (Research Report of the Society of Antiquaries of London).

[18] C. F. C. Hawkes, 'Prehistoric Lincolnshire', *Archaeological Journal*, ciii (1946), p. 14.

[19] *Antiquaries Journal*, xxxix (1959), p. 19.

[20] *British Museum Guide to Early Iron Age Antiquities*, 1925, Figs. 113, 114, and 115.

[21] E. T. Leeds, *Celtic Ornament*, 1933, Fig. 3.

[22] Carried out by Mr. and Mrs. W. T. Jones for the Ministry of Works.

[23] A. L. F. Rivet, *Town and Country in Roman Britain*, 1958, p. 48.

[24] *Antiquaries Journal*, xviii (1938), p. 262.

[25] A suggestion by Prof. W. F. Grimes, *Aspects of Archaeology*, p. 169.

[26] Muriel and Brian Stanley, 'The Defences of the Iron Age Camp at Wappenbury, Warwickshire', *Birmingham Archaeological Society Trans.*, 76 (1958), p. 1.

[27] B. R. Hartley, *Cambridge Antiquarian Society Proceedings*, l (1956–57), pp. 1–27. In the first phase, the outer ditch was 15 ft. deep and 18 ft. wide. Later, when it was recut, its width was almost doubled, and although it was not quite so deep, a counterscarp bank added to its effectiveness. The inner ditch was 38 ft. wide and 17 ft. deep and the rampart was estimated to have been 16 ft. high and 33 ft. wide and its front was supported by a timber palisade. Between the two ditches was another timber-revetted rampart. Only the outer rampart and outer ditch were found to have two phases of construction, so in their original form they must have provided the first defences enclosing about fifteen acres. In the second phase another ditch was added on the inside and a new rampart built, on ground covered with evidence of occupation. The first rampart rests on undisturbed soil.

[28] This is very evident from Fox's Map III in his *Archaeology of the Cambridge Region*, 1923.

[29] T. C. Lethbridge, 'Burial of an Iron Age Warrior at Snailwell', *Cambridge Antiquarian Society Proceedings*, xlvii (1953), p. 25.

[30] *Archaeological Journal*, xcvi (1939), p. 54.

Notes

[31] This is a suggestion made to me by Mr. Derek Allen.

[32] T. G. E. Powell, *The Celts*, 1958, Pls. 49 and 50; H. Schoppa, *Die Kunst der Römerzeit*, Pls. 5 and 13.

[33] 'Belgic Coins as illustrations of Life in the Late Pre-Roman Iron Age of Britain', by Derek Allen, *Proceedings Prehistoric Society*, xxiv (1958), p. 43.

[34] *Antiquity*, xxxiii (1959), Pl. xviii (a).

[35] 'The Carnyx in Early Iron Age Britain', *Antiquaries Journal*, xxxix (1959), p. 19.

[36] S. Piggott, *Prehistoric Society Proceedings*, xvi (1950), pp. 1–28.

[37] *The Stanwick Fortifications*, 1954, p. 53 (Research Report of the Society of Antiquaries of London).

[38] *De rebus bellicis*, translated and discussed by E. A. Thompson, *A Roman Reformer and Inventor*, 1952.

[39] *Antiquaries Journal*, xxvii (1947), p. 117.

Chapter 2

[1] The best work on the subject in English is *The Roman Legions*, by H. M. D. Parker, originally published in 1928 but reissued in 1958.

[2] G. L. Cheesman, *The Auxilia of the Roman Imperial Army*, 1914, remains the only work on the subject in English.

[3] 'The Feriale Duranum', published by R. O. Fink, A. S. Hoey, and W. F. Snyder in *Yale Classical Studies*, vii, 1940. A revised account appears in the excavation report C. B. Welles, R. O. Fink, and J. F. Gilliam, *The Excavations at Dura-Europos*, v. 1. The Parchments and Papyri 1959. This valuable report also includes a daily duty roster with details of duties for each man which throws a vivid light on the army such as could never be obtained from excavations and historical texts alone.

[4] The Greek text has been edited by A. G. Roos, Leipzig, 1907–28, but an English translation remains to be published.

[5] The Ribchester helmet is now in the British Museum, *Antiquities of Roman Britain*, 1951, Pl. xxv, No. 4. The Newstead helmets are in the National Museum of Antiquities, Edinburgh, *A Roman Frontier Post and its People*, 1911, Pls. xxvii-xxx. For an illustration of the Cirencester tombstone see *Archaeologia*, 69, Fig. 13, p. 186.

[6] J. Keim and H. Klumbach, *Der Römische Schatzfund von Straubing*, 1951.

[7] See von Petrikovits, 'Troiaritt und Geranostanz' in *Beiträge zur älteren Europäischen Kultur Geschichte*, Festschift für Rudolf Egger, i, p. 126.

[8] *Cambridge Ancient History*, xii, p. 47. The *Constitutio Antoniniana* has been much discussed by scholars and varying conclusions reached as to its precise effect; see M. Rostovtzeff, *The Social and Economic History of the Roman Empire*, 1957, p. 418, and note on p. 719.

[9] Dr. J. K. St. Joseph has published the results of his surveys in the *Journal of Roman Studies*, xliii (1953), p. 81; xlv (1955), p. 82, and xlviii (1958), p. 86.

[10] For examples of the marching-camp in Britain see I. A. Richmond, 'The Romans in Redesdale' in the *History of Northumberland*, xv, 1940, and I. A. Richmond and J. McIntyre, 'The Roman Camps at Reycross and

Notes

Crackenthorp' in *Trans. Cumberland and Westmorland Antiq. and Arch. Soc.*, xxxiv (1934), p. 50. In the same volume there is a very valuable account of the tents of the Roman Army by the same authors (p. 62). See also O. G. S. Crawford, *Topography of Roman Scotland*, 1949.

[11] Reported in the *Vereeniging voor Terpenonderzoek*. Even the contents of latrine pits were found preserved and put into barrels for study; unfortunately during the war, wood was so scarce in Holland that they were used for firewood and a wonderful opportunity for research into military diet was lost.

[12] This has been skilfully demonstrated by Mr. C. E. Stevens in his paper 'Britain between the Invasions (54 B.C.–A.D. 43): A Study in Ancient Diplomacy' in *Aspects of Archaeology in Britain and Beyond*, 1951 (Essays presented to O. G. S. Crawford), p. 332.

[13] Our information about this battle and the whole campaign is very meagre and derived entirely from the Greek historian Dio Cassius. Unfortunately the relevant books of the *Annals* by Tacitus are missing. Dio's account has been closely studied and a very reasonable account of the Medway battle worked out by A. R. Burn in *History*, xxxix (1953), p. 105.

[14] Parts of this important site have been excavated and published by C. F. C. Hawkes and M. R. Hull, *Camulodunum*, 1947 (Research Report of the Society of Antiquaries of London).

[15] R. E. M. Wheeler, *Maiden Castle, Dorset*, 1943 (Research Report of the Society of Antiquaries of London), Pl. lviii. A.

[16] For the importance of this great limestone belt see the paper by W. F. Grimes, 'The Jurassic Way' in *Aspects of Archaeology in Britain and Beyond*, p. 144.

[17] This is best seen on the Ordnance Survey's *Map of Roman Britain*, 1956.

[18] *Roman Britain and the English Settlements*, 1937, p. 91. For a more recent study of this frontier and the campaigns under Scapula see Graham Webster, 'The Roman Military Advance under Ostorius Scapula' in the *Archaeological Journal*, cxv (1958), p. 49.

[19] 'Britain under Nero: The Significance of Q. Veranius' in *Roman Britain and the Roman Army*, 1953, p. 1, originally appearing in the *Durham University Journal*, 1952, p. 88.

[20] This stamped tile is a problem. There seems little doubt that it reads LVIII (retrograde) (see illustration in *Archaeological Journal* (1918), lxxv, Pl. v, A) which was expanded by Haverfield to Legio VIII, a reading which has been accepted by scholars since. There are also records of two officers of this legion being decorated by Claudius for their part in the British war (*Inscriptiones Latinae Selectae*, 967 and 2701, and CIL, v, 7003) and a draft was evidently included in the invasion force. The difficulty is that there are no other military tiles of this period. The three known legionary fortresses at Lincoln, Gloucester and Wroxeter have not produced a single stamped tile of unchallengeable provenance. One wonders if it could simply be the number 58 and comparable to the two tiles, one from Bath and the other in Berkeley Church, Glos., which read DCLVI.

[21] The most likely place, a flat-topped plateau on the west side of the Derwent, has been built over. Claudian and early Flavian coins have

been found in Strutts Park, near here. (*Derbyshire Arch. Soc. J.*, xlix, p. 355.)

²² The situation in this area is complicated by the recent discovery that the territory west of the Severn was held by the Roman Army well into the second century. To the Leintwardine military complex (S. C. Stanford, 'Excavations at the Roman Camp of Bravonium' in *Woolhope Club Trans.*, xxxvi (1958), p. 87, and 'The Roman Fort at Buckton', ibid., xxxvi (1959), p. 210) must be added the fort at Walltown, Cleobury Mortimer (proved by excavation in 1960), and there must be other forts waiting discovery.

Chapter 3

¹ CIL, vi, 920 (Dessau, 216); CIL, III, s. 7061 (Dessau, 217) Cyzicus.

² Suetonius. *Caligula*, 44. 2.

³ For client-kings see CAH, x, pp. 600 f.; G. H. Stevenson, *Roman Provincial Administration* (Oxford, 1939), ch. II.

⁴ See further Stevenson, op. cit., pp. 43 ff.

⁵ CIL, vii, 11.

⁶ *Annals*, xii, 32.

⁷ For Claudian colonies see V. Scramuzza, *The Emperor Claudius* (Harvard, 1940), pp. 143–4, 196.

⁸ Virgil, *Eclogues*, I 69 ff.; ix, 4 ff.

⁹ Suetonius, *Nero*, 18: cf. E. B. Birley, *Roman Britain and the Roman Army*, p. 7.

¹⁰ Information from Lady Briscoe.

¹¹ For his career see PIR, S. 278; PW, iv A, 591–3.

¹² Tacitus says that in the year 69 he was 'the oldest of the ex-consuls', which would imply, at least, a man of 70.

¹³ On provincial taxation see CAH, x, pp. 196 f.; G. H. Stevenson, op. cit., pp. 150 f.

¹⁴ *Agricola*, 13, i.

¹⁵ *Epitome* of Bk. LXII, 2.

¹⁶ *Annals*, xiv, 31.

¹⁷ *Epitome* of Bk. LXII, 2.

¹⁸ For the Druids, see V. Scramuzza, op. cit., 206–9, and notes.

¹⁹ Tacitus, *Histories*, iv, 54.

²⁰ *Epitome* of Bk. LXII, 3, 4.

²¹ For Vercingetorix see Caesar, *De Bello Gallico*, vii: C. Jullian, *Vercingetorix* (1921).

²² *Agricola*, 15.

²³ *Agricola*, 29, 3.

²⁴ *Chester Archaeological Society*, xxxviii (1951), p. 18.

Chapter 4

¹ Probably before he left Suetonius would have given instructions to burn the corn in the public granaries. He could not take it with him, and would not want it to get into the hands of the Britons. If he did so—here

Notes

and at St. Albans—it was an action that was to have important repercussions later in the campaign.

² Dr. Anne Ross, of the School of Scottish Studies at Edinburgh University, has very kindly supplied the following note:

'Andrasta's name seems to mean something like "the unconquerable", She may have affinities with Andarta, a goddess of the Voconces. Her cult is not referred to elsewhere, but this is usually the case with Celtic deities. The multiplicity of deity names impresses people immediately when they become interested in Celtic religion, as does the extremely limited nature of their functions. Function seems to have been more or less universal, and one may speak of god-types rather than of individual deities. It seems that the names for the various deities changed from area to area while the functions of the different gods were more or less the same. Only in a few cases do we see traces of anything approaching a pantheon, where the actual name has a wide geographical distribution. Again, we know from Old Irish sources that one deity may be known by several different names, for example, the Dagda "the Good God", known also as Eochaid Ollathair "Eochaid, Great Father", and in Ruad Ro-fhessa "Lord of Great Knowledge". Andrasta, although her name seemingly does not occur elsewhere, is a very typical Celtic goddess, her type found more or less universally in the Celtic countries. Her name, meaning perhaps "the invincible" can be paralleled by the names of other great Celtic goddesses. For example, Brigantia "the High One", "Queen", powerful goddess of the Brigantes; Riannon, from Rigantona "Great Queen"; Setlocenia "The Long-Lived One" whose name appears in a dedication from Maryport (Alauna), Cumberland; Ratis "Goddess of the Fortress", implying military associations; the supernatural warrior queen of Old Irish tradition Medb "Intoxication". Finally, the trio of war/fertility goddesses from Ireland must be considered as having been closely similar to Andrasta. Macha "Crow", Badb-catha "Battle-raven" (found in Gaul as Cathubodya), and Morrigan "Great Queen" or "Queen of Nightmares", all concerned with influencing the outcome of battle by magic, proclaiming victories from the hilltops, foretelling future evil, and having sexual aspects. The great goddess of the Iceni was presumably a goddess such as these, concerned with battle, associated with victory, and her sexual aspects may account for the "wanton behaviour" which Dio refers to.

'This dualism is found very widely in Celtic religion, and the concept of war and fertility (that is death and rebirth) seems to be fundamental. It is perhaps of interest to note that Brigantia, goddess of the Brigantes, becomes, under the influence of *interpretatio Romana*, assimilated to Victory, while a coin of the Cantii shows an unusually fierce and frenzied Victory which Evans has suggested may represent Andrasta herself. The Celtic goddesses, moreover, seem to have been very much bound up with territory, and this may help to account for their extremely local nature. Consequently, although this goddess was clearly of great importance to the Iceni, the fact that she seems to be unknown elsewhere is fully explicable in the light of wider Celtic religious traditions.

'I don't think there is any reason to think Dio's account of the atrocities committed by the Britons is in any way fabricated. Such details as the sewing of the breasts of the women to their mouths may be imaginary, but there are various classical references to the fierce ritual practices of the Celts in Europe, and it is known that the Celts hung people up in trees and sacrificed them to their deities. We also know that heads were impaled on stakes and displayed in prominent places, and in the case of the Iceni, it seems clear that religious rites were being performed in honour of the tribal goddess who was regarded as being responsible for the great victory. The Gauls sacrificed prisoners of war to their gods, and this massacre can probably best be regarded in the light of a great religious sacrifice. Feasts amongst the Celts, moreover, were frequently of a ritual character, and religious gatherings were invariably accompanied by games and banquets and festivities of all kings. It is perhaps significant that Cormac, in his ninth-century Irish glossary, glosses the goddess Macha in the following way. "Macha, that is a crow; that is one of the three morrigans. Mesrad Machae, Mach's mast, that is the heads of men after their slaughter." These heads appear to have been offered up to the goddess after battle as her due. The description of these rites as having been performed in a sacred grove is likewise convincing, and altogether, I see no reason why, apart from perhaps the detail about the breasts, it should not be accepted as it stands, as being a genuine account of mass sacrifice to the war/fertility goddess Andrasta, the name of the powerful tribal goddess of the Iceni.'

[3] It seems impossible to be more precise. The speculation of nearly three centuries has produced many candidates for the site of the battle, but few can be taken seriously. The British antiquary clings firmly to the belief that all historical events can be placed on the map, and that most of them happened in his own county. Essex has always asserted its claims; as, for instance, those of Haynes Green, near Layer Marney, confidently advanced by Jenkins (*Archaeologia*, Vol 29, 1842), and supported by some very farfetched etymology. London has yielded no ground to Essex. A 'tradition' quoted by several antiquaries of the early nineteenth century places the site in Islington; as recently as 1937 this was revived by Lewis Spence, who engagingly places King's Cross Station in the defile occupied by Suetonius. Two German scholars of the first rank, Mommsen and Domaszewski, have taken up the problem, but only to darken council by siting the battle near Chester. The present authors, it will be seen, follow the tradition of the British antiquary.

Chapter 5

[1] *Ann.*, xiv, 39: *Agric.*, 16, 3.
[2] *Ann* , xv, 72.
[3] *Hist.*, 1, 6.
[4] *Agric.*, 16, 4.
[5] *Hist.*, 1, 60.

Notes

6 *Agric.*, 16, 6.

7 Eric Birley, *The Roman Army in Britain* (1953), pp. 13 ff.

8 Probably Trajanic. Illustrated in Rostovtzeff, *History of the Ancient World*: Rome, Pl. LXXVIII.

9 See p. 145.

10 *Agric.*, 19.

11 R. B. Collingwood, *Roman Britain and the English Settlements*, p. 104.

12 *Agric.*, 19.

13 For Augustodunum see O. Brogan, *Roman Gaul*, pp. 44, 68–69, 223–4. For the schools see T. J. Haarhoff, *Schools of Gaul* (Johannesburg, 1958), pp. 33 ff.

14 *Ann.*, iii, 43.

15 For Trèves see O. Brogan, op. cit., pp. 111–16.

16 *Ann.*, xi, 19. cf. J. J. Hatt, *Histoire de la Gaule Romaine* (Paris, 1959), p. 129.

17 A. L. F. Rivet, *Town and Country in Roman Britain* (London, 1958), p. 61.

18 Quoted in A. R. Burn, *Agricola and Roman Britain*, pp. 66–67.

19 K. H. Jackson, *Language and History in Early Britain* (Edinburgh, 1953), see especially chapter III.

20 This seems the most likely period for the writing of his *Memoirs*. Earlier, scholars have assumed that they could only refer to the African campaigns because (*a*) the fragments are all about Mauretania (the wild animals of the vanished Forest of Guair, etc.), (*b*) the African campaigns were successful, the British chequered, and so the *Memoirs* could only be concerned with the former. To those familiar with the memoirs of the generals of the Second World War, this argument will seem somewhat less than convincing.

21 For the later stages of his career, see *Hist.*, i, 87, 90: ii, 23–26, 31, 33, 37, 39, 40, 44, 60.

22 He escapes from the patrols of Vitellius, disguised as a peasant (*Hist.*, iii, 59, 3), from an enemy night attack on his headquarters, through being away visiting his mistress (*Hist.*, v, 21, 3).

23 There is a full account in CAH, x, pp. 842 ff. See also J. J. Hatt, op. cit., pp. 144 ff. Tacitus's account begins in *Hist.*, ix, 12; and see L. Hammand, *l'Occident Romain* (Paris, 1960), pp. 168 ff.

24 *Hist.*, iv, 54.

25 *Hist.*, iv, 61.

26 *Hist.*, ii, 61.

27 For these men see R. Syme, *Tacitus* (Oxford, 1958), pp. 173, 461–2, 456 n.

28 See R. Syme, op. cit., 453.

29 *Hist.*, iv, 58, 59.

30 *Hist.*, iv, 71.

31 *Hist.*, iv, 73. See discussion in R. Syme, op. cit., pp. 441, 453, 529.

32 For Cerialis's advance to the north, see Eric Birley, op. cit., pp. 11 f., 17 f., 39 ff.

Notes

[33] 'imponite quinquaginta annis magnum diem' (at the battle of Mons Graupius), *Agric.*, 34.

[34] Britain as *'ferox provincia'*, *Agric.*, 8.

Chapter 6

[1] *Journal of Roman Studies*, xxxi (1941), p. 37.

[2] 'Two Fires of Roman London', *Antiquaries Journal*, xxv (1945), p. 48.

[3] *Archaeologia*, lxii; (1911–12), Pl. lvi; *Royal Commission on Historical Monuments, Roman London*, 1928, Fig. 24.

[4] *London in Roman Times* (1930), Pl. ii.

[5] M. R. Hull, *Roman Colchester*, 1958, p. 153 (Research Report of the Society of Antiquaries of London).

[6] *Trans. Essex Archaeological Society*, xix, p. 277; xx, p. 211.

[7] *Roman Colchester*, p. 198.

[8] Ibid., p. 104.

[9] Ibid., p. 148.

[10] This church, which had been almost entirely rebuilt in 1875, was demolished in 1955 to make way for a store. Here and there were found clay walls and traces of destruction, also fragments of fine stucco facings of large columns similar to those found in the drain in front of the temple (see below, note 13).

[11] *Journal of Roman Studies*, ix (1919), p. 139; x (1920), p. 87.

[12] *Roman Colchester*, Figs. 83 and 84.

[13] M. R. Hull, 'The South Wing of the Roman "Forum" at Colchester, recent discoveries', *Essex Archaeological Society Trans.*, xxv (1955), p. 24.

[14] C. F. C. Hawkes and M. R. Hull, *Camulodunum*, 1947.

[15] *Camulodunum*, p. 40.

[16] Ibid., p. 43.

[17] *Roman Colchester*, Pl. 1.

[18] M. R. Hull, 'A Roman Tombstone found in Colchester', *Essex Archaeological Society Trans.*, xix, p. 117.

[19] George Macdonald, 'Note on some fragments of Imperial statues and of a statuette of Victory', *Journal of Roman Studies*, xvi (1926), p. 1; Prof. J. M. C. Toynbee, 'Some notes on Roman Art at Colchester', *Essex Archaeological Society Trans.*, xxv (1955), p. 10; *Roman Colchester*, Frontispiece. A bronze head found in the River Waal, near Nijmegen, with very similar hairstyle has been identified as Trajan by van Buchem (*Bulletin van de Vereeniging tot bevordering der Kennis van de Antieke Beschaving*, xxxi, 1956), and this suggests caution in accepting the Alde head as being definitely that of Claudius.

[20] *Athenaeum* report on a meeting of the Society of Antiquaries, 3rd December 1908.

[20a] Reported in *The Times*, 9th Feb., 1962.

[21] R. E. M. and T. V. Wheeler, *Verulamium, A Belgic and two Roman Cities*, 1936 (Research Report of the Society of Antiquaries of London).

Notes

[22] S. S. Frere, 'Excavations at Verulamium 1956', *Antiquaries Journal,* xxxvii (1957), p. 4.

[23] S. S. Frere, 'Excavations at Verulamium 1955', *Antiquaries Journal,* xxxvi (1956), p. 5.

[23a] S. S. Frere, 'Excavations at Verulamium 1958', *Antiquaries Journal,* xxxix (1959), p. 3.

[24] 'The Legionary Fortress at Lincoln', *Journal of Roman Studies,* xxxix (1949), p. 57.

[25] The probable existence of this fort had been brought to light by excavations on the later Roman town (*The Roman Town and Villa at Great Casterton, Rutland,* 1957, p. 14). It was not, however, actually discovered until 1959, when it was observed from the air immediately to the east of the town by Dr. J. K. St. Joseph. Trial excavations took place in Easter 1960 under the direction of Professor I. A. Richmond and Dr. Philip Corder, and we are grateful to them for this information prior to publication.

[26] This may represent only a tenth of the original deposit, part of which may still be lying in the undisturbed peat.

[27] *A Find of the Early Iron Age from Llyn Cerrig Bach, Anglesey,* 1946. (The book was not actually published until May 1947.)

[28] Strabo, 4, 1, 13.

[29] A cuirass hinge and lunate pendant in the Castle Museum, Norwich, from the former, and part of a decorated belt in the British Museum from the latter. It would be very difficult to distinguish between Roman military activities under Scapula in A.D. 48 and those of A.D. 60. This also applies to native resistance. The site at Thornham (53/726425) has, for example, produced evidence of a possible native fortification in the Roman style associated with material of mid-first-century date, but unless a critical coin or a piece of decorated samian could also be found it would be impossible to place this work securely in its correct historical context.

[30] *Norfolk and Norwich Archaeological Society,* xxiv (1931), p. 133.

Chapter 7

[1] *Agricola,* 46.

[2] Gildas, *De Excidio Britanniae,* c.6. Translation by Giles, *The Works of Gildas and Nennius* (London, 1841), p. 9.

[3] *Dictionary of Welsh Biography,* s.v. 'Gildas'.

[4] Bede, *Historia Ecclesiastica,* I, 3.

[5] J. S. P. Tatlock, *The Legendary History of Britain* (Berkley, 1950), pp. 426–7.

[6] For Polydore Vergil and the British history see T. D. Kendrick, *British Antiquity* (London, 1949), pp. 79 f.

[7] Polydore Vergil, *Anglica Historia,* translation of Books i–viii by Sir Henry Ellis, *Camden Society,* 1846.

[8] For Hector Boëce see T. D. Kendrick, op. cit., pp. 65 f.

[9] T. D. Kendrick, op. cit., pp. 135–6.

Notes

¹⁰ Camden, *Britannia*. This is the source for the appearance of 'Bunduca' in Spenser's poem *The Ruines of Time*, and *Faerie Queene* (Bk. II, Canto X), and also in Ben Jonson's *The Masque of Queenes*, played in 1609.

¹¹ Shakespeare, *Cymbeline*, Act V, v.

¹² Stephen Gosson, *The School of Abuse*, containing a pleasant invective against Poets, Pipers, Jesters, and suchlike Caterpillers of a Commonwealth: Setting up the Flagge of Defiance to their mischievous exercise, and over-throwing their Bulwarks, by Prophane Writers, Natural reason, and common experience (1579).

¹³ s.v. *Dictionary of National Biography*, 'Ubaldini'.

¹⁴ cf. the article on *Bonduca* by Leonhardt in *Englische Studien*, xiii, pp. 36 f.

¹⁵ The historical Caratacus appears in *The Valiant Welshman*. (The true chronicles of the life and valiant deeds of Caradoc the Great, King of Cambria, now called Wales), by R. A. Gent, 1615.

¹⁶ *Bonduca*, Act III, sc. V.

¹⁷ *Bonduca*, Act III, sc. V. *2nd Daughter* By—Uncle

> We will have vengeance for our rapes.

Caratach   By—
> You should have kept your legs close then . . .

¹⁸ *Bonduca*, Act IV, sc. V.

¹⁹ Another Romano-British theme at about this period is the *Caratacus* of William Mason (*c.* 1750).

²⁰ Milton had read the British historians in 1641–2.

²¹ T. D. Kendrick, *The Druids* (London, 1927): Stuart Piggott, *William Stukeley* (Oxford, 1950), ch. IV.

²² *Nero Caesar*, or *Monarchie Depraved*. An Historical Work (1624), p. 181. For the 'Academ Royal' see Joan Evans, *A History of the Society of Antiquaries* (Oxford, 1956), pp. 17, 18.

²³ For Sammes see T. D. Kendrick, *British Antiquity*, 76, 133.

²⁴ See RCHM, Middlesex.

²⁵ Stuart Piggott, op. cit., p. 54.

²⁶ Horsley, *Britannia Romana*, p. 28.

²⁷ David Hume, *History of England* (Ed. Warne, 1884), vol. i, p. 4.

²⁸ Charles Tennyson, *Memoirs*, p. 323.

²⁹ *Anthologia Latina* (ed. Riese), Vol. I, 426.

³⁰ For Thornycroft and the history of the project see Elfrida Thorny-croft, *Bronze and Steel*—The Life of Thomas Thornycroft, Sculptor and Engineer (The King's Stone Press, 1932), pp. 56–57, 62, 70 f. For the completed group see Lord Edward Gleichen, *London's Open-Air Statuary* (London, 1928), pp. 97–98.

³¹ Op. cit., p. 216.

³² Op. cit., pp. 18–23.

INDEX

Index

Index

Index